T0022721

Gender History: A Very Short Introduction

VERY SHORT INTRODUCTIONS are for anyone wanting a stimulating and accessible way into a new subject. They are written by experts, and have been translated into more than 45 different languages.

The series began in 1995, and now covers a wide variety of topics in every discipline. The VSI library currently contains over 750 volumes—a Very Short Introduction to everything from Psychology and Philosophy of Science to American History and Relativity—and continues to grow in every subject area.

## Very Short Introductions available now:

**Available soon:**

For more information visit our website

www.oup.com/vsi/

Antoinette Burton

# GENDER HISTORY

## A Very Short Introduction

## OXFORD
UNIVERSITY PRESS

Oxford University Press is a department of the University of Oxford.
It furthers the University's objective of excellence in research, scholarship,
and education by publishing worldwide. Oxford is a registered trade mark of
Oxford University Press in the UK and in certain other countries.

Published in the United States of America by Oxford University Press
198 Madison Avenue, New York, NY 10016, United States of America.

Library of Congress Cataloging-in-Publication Data

Names: Burton, Antoinette M., 1961- author.
Title: Gender history : a very short introduction / Antoinette Burton.
Description: New York, NY : Oxford University Press, [2024] | Series:
Very short introductions | Includes bibliographical references and index.
Identifiers: LCCN 2023046866 (print) | LCCN 2023046867 (ebook) |
ISBN 9780197587010 (paperback) | ISBN 9780197587034 (epub)
Subjects: LCSH: Sex role—History. | Sex discrimination—History. |
Feminism—History. | Gender identity—History.
Classification: LCC HQ1075 .B876 2024 (print) | LCC HQ1075 (ebook) |
DDC 305.309—dc23/eng/20231019
LC record available at https://lccn.loc.gov/2023046866
LC ebook record available at https://lccn.loc.gov/2023046867

Integrated Books International, United States of America

# Contents

# List of illustrations

# Introduction: Gender history in context

When people think of gender history, they are likely to imagine a particular kind of academic work, involving scholarly books and articles that make ideas about masculinity and femininity evident in all kinds of times and places in order to tell a story of difference, discrimination, struggle, and visibility, and of equality "between the sexes." And that would certainly be right. Gender history has been an academic field since the 1970s. It has several well-established journals, an intergenerational array of award-winning practitioners, and an equally impressive bibliography that addresses the role that gender has played in shaping histories from the Neolithic period to the present. It has been a global phenomenon as well. Historians who work in and write about virtually every quarter of the planet have tackled the question of what gender has meant in their societies and what impact its histories have had, right down to the present. Even its critics will admit that, together with women's history, gender history has been one of the most significant developments in the discipline since World War II.

The history of gender—in law, as culture, and through identity politics—is an enduring, powerful provocation on both the global stage and in everyday life. One has only to think of how we talk about gender history when we talk about the comedian Lucille Ball, the Black women scientists in the film *Hidden Figures*, the future of the workforce, or historic "firsts" like the election of Angela Merkel in Germany or Kamala Harris in the United States. Narratives of gender history can be found, too, in the rise of autocrats and in sports culture, whether we are talking about Benito Mussolini or Rodrigo Duterte, FIFA management or transgender athletes. While conversations like these are not the focus of this book, such common examples remind us that gender history is not merely an academic question: it matters in consequential ways to every arena of public and private life, the world over.

This volume is designed to introduce the scholarly field of gender history: its origins, development, reception, recalibrations, and frictions. It offers a set of working definitions of gender as a descriptive category and as a category of historical analysis, tracing the emergence, usage, and applicability of these entwined subjects across a range of times and places in the scholarship since the 1980s. Inevitably political, gender history has taken aim at the broader field of historical narrative by asking who counts as a historical subject and what difference gender difference makes. It has also been concerned with how attention to gender in history subverts reigning assumptions of what power, culture, economics, and identity have been in the past—with ramifications, of course, for what they are today. Now widely recognized as a key component of historical methodology, gender history and the first gender historians struggled for acceptance *as historians*. That may seem remarkable today, but it reminds us of the precarious place from which the field began, and, of course, of its relative newness in the long historical scheme of things.

Because gender history takes shape (like all history, in fact) in tense and tender relationship to the times it inhabits, any introduction to it must grapple with the fact that the very centrality and stability of its key category, gender itself, has been in question across its whole history as a field. Scholars of class and race and ethnicity have challenged the isolation of gender from other axes of identity, calling for an intersectional approach to both the study of gender and its work in the world. Queer and transgender scholars, themselves shaped by racial and social difference and often influenced by poststructuralist thinking, have questioned the binaries that can undergird gender history, asking us to appreciate gender not as fixed or original but as constantly troubled, and as continuously performed in specific contexts. What is intriguing and ultimately defining about gender history is how and why it has run up against voices and forces that take exception to the singularity, and the sovereignty, of gender itself as an explanatory category. These powerful, unruly tensions are at the heart of this *Very Short Introduction*. And they suggest some of the ways that gender history has channeled wider crises of political and cultural authority since it took hold as a disciplinary field.

Over the course of several decades of teaching gender history, I have often been struck by the linear progressive narrative through which the interrelated components of the field are recounted. Students and even some faculty colleagues tend to imagine that women's history, with its recuperative, "compensatory" impulse, came first, and that gender history, with a more sophisticated analytical lens, followed. Then came intersectional critique from Black women and scholars of color; and now, in the wake of queer and trans histories, which have (it is said) blown up gender as our grandmothers knew it, we have moved to the most progressive plane of all. As viewed from 10,000 feet and run through an unselfconsciously liberal approach to political change, this might seem a reasonable take. Indeed, such an approach is effectively pegged to assumptions about the historical relationship of women's movements to civil rights to marriage equality to LGBTQ+—that is, they happened one after the other, with key moments of connectivity, perhaps, but serially and in progressive fashion nonetheless.

1. **Evidence of how the gender binary shapes daily life is everywhere. Vintage toilet signs from the Victorian underground in Glasgow, photographed in 2014, evoke a time when the segregation of "Gents" from "Ladies" was the norm in public spaces.**

There have undoubtedly been consequential shifts and changes in how we think and write about the past as a result of how gender history as a field has emerged. Yet progress is at once too easy and too glib a description of how and why this is so. One goal of this book is to dispel the notion that gender history has either ridden or driven an arc of progressive development. For one thing, gender history has always been embedded in and cross-hatched by a combination of research and teaching that questioned the primacy of gender itself—questioning produced in the *shared* context of women's liberation, civil rights, LGBTQ+, and decolonization movements of the late twentieth century. By the same token, gender history has not surpassed lesser forms of practice nor been superseded by superior forms of radical history-writing. Born of a specific set of left-liberal scholar-activist formations, the field of gender history is one expression of the histories out of which it comes: one change agent—albeit an important one—among many. The vibrancy of gender history in all its plurality today is fed in

4

part by the investment so many people continue to have in the power of gender and the power of history combined to illuminate social and political crises, in the past and in the present. Its archive of insights and its ever-adaptive methodologies (even when flawed) mean that gender history remains critical to all dimensions of historical practice, whether inside or beyond the discipline of history per se.

What I have described so far will sound like a very Western story and, in fact, a very white middle-class North American perspective. It is important to recognize that movements for gender equality were (and are) thought to be key to modern Western progress—progress identified by some with the "American Century," typically periodized as the era of US hegemony after 1945. Gender history as a field has been caught up in the domestic and international politics of that extended moment. One of the leading scholars of the field, Joan Scott, is an American historian of France who has challenged the border between academic work and political life, such as when she appeared as an expert in the legal case brought by working women against the Sears Roebuck corporation, or when she published her work on the Muslim veil, linking its ban in France to the failed politics of postcolonial assimilation. It is arguably a testimony to her influence (and that of other scholars) that American gender theory is so vilified in Europe as a kind of American contamination, and not only by right-leaning regimes. In this context, gender history, as one aspect of global conversations about how gender can and should work, is a lightning rod for an array of geopolitical debates and crises.

Accounts of gender history that point to its white, middle-class, and Western origins are readily available, thanks to radical women of color—Angela Davis, Hazel Carby, Gloria Anzaldúa, Cherríe Moraga, Chandra Mohanty, bell hooks, to name only a few—who posed antiracist challenges to mainstream feminism and whose work has circulated globally since the 1960s and 1970s. Yet this troubling history may come as a surprise to readers unaccustomed to thinking of gender history as a predominantly Western phenomenon, and also to those who assume history itself as a discipline is untouched by geopolitics, especially of the inheritances of modern racism and imperialism. Meanwhile, for some scholars working through the practices of gender history, the question has arisen as to whether gender is anything like an organic concept outside Euro-American society, let alone beyond its academic institutions and its professional organs of dissemination. Given that, in demographic terms, the vast majority of its practitioners reside in the United States and Europe, gender history as a field continues to reflect many of the struggles that have characterized the twentieth-century histories from which it has emerged.

Gender history has not been immune, then, from the imprint of either US politics or Western colonial legacies, and its social life as an intellectual formation has been rife with challenges. Those challenges have come from Black, Brown, and Indigenous scholars in the United States and from those from former colonial societies. They question not simply the singularity of gender, but equally its legitimacy as an analytic, because of its historical emergence in and through the very warp and weave of colonial and postcolonial histories—because of the ways that binaries of gender can themselves be so bound up in imperial histories. And because history as a Western discipline thinks most often through the time of the modern, the temporality of gender history has been an issue as well. That is, scholars working in ancient, precolonial, and premodern periods worry about the modernist biases that gender history methodology carries, to such a degree that the "gender" in gender history can, if we are not mindful, be construed as a Trojan horse for a plethora of ahistorical interpretations.

Beyond its accomplishments, its struggles for recognition, and its limitations, gender history is hardly innocent of the historical conditions that engendered it. As a scholarly field, it offers ample evidence of the limits of the march-of-progress storyline in which it is often situated. Given the rise of fascist and right-wing politics globally, it is surely time for the fantasy of modern liberal progress, whether in politics or the development of historical fields, to be punctured. I read gender history not as a site of progress but as a field of inquiry that is symptomatic of the many crises (social, political, methodological) out of which it developed and in which it continues to operate. My goal is to get, and keep, gender history out of isolation so that we acknowledge the various conditions that have generated, and will continue to sustain, its work.

I use three strategies toward this end. First, I make visible the field's historical and ongoing connections to arenas like women's and queer history in an effort to refuse the progressive destiny that is often implied about its trajectory. Second, where possible, I seek to recall the social movement contexts in which and out of which gender history emerged, in the United States and beyond. That kind of overtly political connection, by the way, partly accounts for why gender is eschewed, especially by scholars who prefer their histories to be above the "fray" of politics. And finally, I'm interested in how and why gender history is hardly limited to the confines of academe. As a way of thinking about the past that prioritizes a range of identities rooted in notions of male and female without seeing them as timeless or essential, gender history and the stories it tells are everywhere in contemporary culture, the world over. As a lens for rethinking conventional accounts of politics, the social, economics, religion, labor, and even History (with a capital H) itself, gender history is a resource for everything from the #MeToo movement to alt-right conspiracies, struggles against global capital, Black Lives Matter, or a stand-up comedy act such as Hannah Gadsby's *Nanette*.

I make a distinction here between gender history and gender studies. The latter is an interdisciplinary field often institutionalized in academic departments, and sometimes organized adjacent to ethnic studies or other interrelated units in spaces of Western higher education. The former typically has no given institutional home. Its practitioners may be in history departments or in gender studies programs. Academic jobs advertised as gender history are rarer than ever (as are jobs in women's history), though positions in queer or trans or Indigenous or Latina/o studies may include references to gender history as part of their remit. At the same time, the "history" in gender history can be misleading, for its practitioners often draw on multiple inter/disciplinary approaches (as do most practicing historians in any case) even as they think about the contingency of time and place as a major structuring lens for interpretation and explanation. Evidence and archives—these remain critical, though the way such sites are themselves seen to be steeped in the presumptions and values of the past that gender historians are often invested in upending remains a productive tension in the field. But even in its most radical forms, gender history valorizes methods and practices that try to capture the ways that, as the editorial collective of the journal *Gender and History* put it in 1989, "the creation and reproduction of gender is a [historical] *process*," unfolding in the specific conditions of any given moment(s) and place(s).

Now to my own position in relation to the field of gender history. As a white US-based feminist historian of modern British imperialism who has done work on South Asia, South Africa, and empire "at home," focusing on women, race, the global, and, most recently, animal worlds, my training as a researcher and my experience as a teacher inform every aspect of my approach to the subject. As does the time of my emergence as a historian: born in 1961 and having earned a PhD in history in the United States in 1990, I am a cisgender scholar who came of age intellectually and politically just as the powerful combination of decolonization and feminism was shaping the ways that history was done, the ways that gender was mobilized—and, frankly, the ways that the Anglo-American world order of the pre-1940 era was experiencing a global crisis. I do not have a complete sense of how those histories shaped me, but I do know they have afforded me a set of convictions about how gender works and what history is capable of doing. In keeping with the expectations of the field of gender history that partially made me, I acknowledge the subjective, if nonetheless rigorous and principled, character of my approach here. I'm also skeptical about the possibility of objective, disinterested study—a posture with which my long-standing engagements with women's, feminism, and empire history have equipped me. As a child of the historical conditions and crises that have given rise to gender history, it could not be otherwise. As a reader, I would ask you in the same spirit: Where do you locate yourself in these histories?

As a field, gender history has been extraordinarily influential in shaping several generations of scholars and students, myself included. More conspicuously, perhaps, the eruption of queer and transgender communities into the socially mediated public sphere over the course of the last half century has made gender newly available to many as a way of talking about identity, belonging, alienation, and history, too. Some of the same historical conditions and struggles that have made that emergence possible have also made gender history—the story of how male and female came to be understood as a pairing, a binary, and what that undoing can or should look like—a powerful political, economic, and cultural resource for individuals and collectivities alike. In that sense, "gender history" might be said to be hiding in plain sight, at work everywhere we look. A clear-eyed grasp of how gender history arrived as an academic field is certainly important for understanding how research and teaching in the humanities, the social sciences, and beyond have been shaped since the late twentieth century. Even more consequentially, appreciating the ways that gender history lives in the world is key to unlocking what our experiences of contemporary life may mean for us, and for whatever comes next.

# Chapter 1
# Some origins of gender history as a field

The year 1989 was a monumental one. The Berlin Wall fell. Protesters occupied Tiananmen Square. The Loma Prieta earthquake, magnitude 6.9, disrupted the World Series. The Soviet-Afghan War ended. The first GMO trial was launched. South Africa held its last election under apartheid. The rap group N.W.A.'s album *Straight Outta Compton* reached one million sales. The Family and Medical Leave Act was reintroduced in the US Senate. The Ayatollah Khomeini issued a fatwa against Salman Rushdie. The first Global Positioning Satellite (GPS) went into orbit. Riots provoked a state of emergency in Argentina. A tornado in Bangladesh killed over 1,300 people. It was the 20th anniversary of Stonewall, and Denmark became the first nation to legalize same-sex unions. Barbara Harris became the first woman bishop in the Anglican Episcopal Church. Francis Fukuyama wrote "The End of History?"

In 1989, no women won Nobel prizes. Margaret Thatcher completed a decade as UK prime minister. Mark Lépine gunned down fourteen women at the University of Montreal Engineering School after shouting "I hate feminists." More than two-thirds of the women in jail in the United States had children under the age of 18. The musical *Miss Saigon* became one of the longest-running shows on Broadway.

In 1989 Lucille Ball (American actress) died. Elena Ceaușescu (Romanian communist) was executed. And *Gender and History* (the first academic journal dedicated to gender history) launched its first issue. The premise of the journal was straightforward. As the founding statement from the editorial collective "Why Gender and History?" proclaimed, the journal "brings to the study of history the centrality of gender relations and to the study of gender a sense of history." The editors sought "to examine all historical social relations from a feminist perspective, to construct a comprehensive analysis of all institutions that takes their gender-specific characters into account. In addressing men and masculinity as well as women and femininity, the journal will illuminate the ways in which societies have been shaped by the relations of power between women and men."

What followed was a powerful case for the work of gender as a site of historical experience, meaning, and significance, and an avowed commitment to examining "all aspects of gender in all places—in the home and in the workplace, in the neighborhood and in diplomacy, in play and in war, in private relations and in parliaments." Attention to the limits of the public-private divide, to the importance of masculinity as a right and proper subject, to interdisciplinary approaches, to histories of all times and places, and to the inclusion of nonprofessional as well as full-time historians—these are the dimensions of what the journal identified as a "gender-oriented approach" to history. In this term-setting context, gender was defined as "not only a set of lived relations" but also "a symbolic system." Here, "symbolic" meant metaphorical, even allegorical: a means of exploring the way that "gender attributes" structure representations of units such as the nation (whether as "motherland" or "fatherland," for example).

At the same time, the editors were keen to make it clear that their project was to bring such forms of descriptive analysis into dialogue with attention to relations of domination and subordination. This articulation of the tension between the representation of gender and its embeddedness in material social relations is significant. It suggests that gender history began its professional life as a bridge between scholars invested in social history and those taking the turn toward discourse, with its emphasis on language as the mediator of power relations and on textual analysis as a means of accessing power dynamics. Sometimes called "the linguistic turn," this emphasis on texts as mineable resources for social and cultural history was a methodological innovation that feminist scholars often championed. As an opportunity to think through interdisciplinarity, it offered the possibility of examining history and its limits when it came to what the historian Kathleen Canning called keywords in the vocabulary of social history— women and gender among them.

Apropos, and unsurprisingly given the journal's title, the discipline of history, its male practitioners, and its resulting male bias came in for scrutiny from the start as well. "For men," the editors wrote, "one of the great privileges of being in a superior position is being allowed to... claim that identity as the norm, and to treat that hierarchy as natural. This is as true for the study of history as it is for the historical past itself. Since it is men who have, by and large, been responsible for the doing and writing of history, it is their definition of the legitimate historical project which has prevailed." Through the exercise of such privilege, "they silence the voices of the less powerful and simultaneously deny a genuine examination of their own dominant position; they celebrate divisions which function both to organize gender relations and to ordain masculinity." This, the editors argued, "must change."

That imperative required not a rejection of men, but rather a gendered history aimed at understanding "how male actors saw their actions as contributing to their positions and resources *as men*, and how such activities defined men as separate from and superior to women and the feminine" (emphasis in the original). Yet for all the sense of balance the editors brought to this opening gambit, they were plain-spoken about the stakes of the work for the profession itself, because, as they observed, "the expanding interest in the place and meaning of women's lives in the past still remains, for the most part, outside the main body of historical writing." What they hoped to accomplish in the journal from the vantage point of 1989 was to bring women and gender—and in many cases, women *as* gender—into the mainstream of history as a professional discipline. And if they fell short of saying that the practice of history would itself be transformed, they insisted, with what I think of as a combination of understatement and cheek, that "gendered history calls for the exercise of the highest degree of historical imagination." That meant not just "seeing women" but recognizing gender ideologies like domesticity, respectability, and white heteronormativity at work.

Notable is the recurrent linkage between women's history and gender history. Indeed, in many ways this first editorial is a microhistory of that ongoing symbiotic relationship—a relationship taking shape in the context of feminism as both a political movement and an intellectual formation. The journal editors pay homage to the work of historians of women whose investigations were shaped by the feminist movement, though they do not name names. It's here that we see the seeds of a progressive narrative of history—women's history first, then gender history—emerging, with gender history expressly associated with more complex ways of thinking. "Many who participated in the early, compensatory phase of women's history are now bringing a similar energy and excitement to challenging wider areas of study," they observed. And "as feminism has developed more sophisticated understandings, academic disciplines have responded with broadened horizons." To be sure, historians of women had laid much groundwork in the 1970s for

**2. In this 1950s image of the ideal modern kitchen, traditional white Western gender roles are on display alongside the newest stove and refrigerator—as is the way that those gender roles are socially reproduced, passing from mother to daughter via middle-class respectability.**

gender as a social relationship. And yet throughout the editorial, and across the whole inaugural issue of *Gender and History*, and despite the nods to the necessity of attending to masculinity, women and gender are more often than not coupled as, together, the right and proper subjects of the change in history writing that's being called for.

What's more, even as gender history as a distinct field of study was being launched in these pages, we are witness to cracks in the argument about the centrality and coherence of gender itself. We are told, for example, that the emphasis of *Gender and History* is on "putting the question of gender at the centre of the historical agenda." But on the very first page of the new journal, that primacy is qualified: "We seek particularly to encourage research not only on gender and women but also on how other divisions—of race, class, religion, ethnicity and sexual orientation—have redounded on both ideas about gender and the experiences of women." Further on, we are told that in some historical times and places, societies have given primacy to identities other than male-female, and that gender is, moreover, "an inherently unstable and contradictory concept." Further still, we learn that gender is "one of the prime forces of historical change"—which, if not exactly a retreat from the "centre of the historical agenda," feels like a qualification of its sovereign role.

Even more remarkably, the editorial begins its enunciation of the contents of the new journal by drawing readers' attention to the fact that an image of Sojourner Truth, "abolitionist and woman's rights advocate," graces the inaugural cover. The editors describe her as "aged and grandmotherly, wrapped in a shawl, performing traditional Victorian womanly work." She is an "abolitionist and woman's rights advocate, bearing children into bondage, wearing an African head dress," and an "illiterate slave, charismatic preacher, advocating the western migration of newly freed blacks. Womanly, feminist, Africanist, manly: our image of her changes with each new perspective." At the 1851 Ohio Woman's Rights Convention, we are told, Sojourner Truth "confronted these contradictions. Detailing a litany of physical labours and abuses she had borne—labours and abuses undiminished by consideration of her sex—she asked, 'Ar'n't I a Woman?'"

This first issue of *Gender and History* pledged to build on Sojourner Truth's simple but profound question. By way of context, the editors explained that "her large frame and deep voice, in conjunction with her black skin and radical views, led opponents to challenge her at every level including her sexual identity." During an 1858 lecture, the editors recount, "a doctor demanded that she 'submit her breasts to the inspection of some ladies' as proof of her womanhood. Truth responded that 'her breasts had suckled many a white babe, to the exclusion of her own offspring and she quietly asked them as she disrobed her bosom, if they, too, wished to suck!' To show her breasts to the whole congregation, she proclaimed, 'was not to her shame,' but to theirs."

The editors of *Gender and History* declared that "as scholars, we, too, seek to provoke and inspire, to make the bold gesture or contribute the daring words that will illuminate the material realities and symbolic powers of womanhood and manhood, femininity and masculinity, sex and sexuality." These passages effectively positioned the field of gender history as a continuation of the work of Sojourner Truth. In so doing, they claimed a black feminist inheritance derived from histories of slavery that are implied rather than named—and, in the process, they (re)produce an image of a formerly enslaved person whose biological womanhood was in question due to the skepticism of professional men (in the person of the anonymous doctor).

As Nell Irvin Painter has detailed, there is significant doubt as to whether Truth ever uttered those now famous words; what is more, she argues, "the false quote flattens Truth into little more than a magical savior of white women." The full content of this historic first issue of the journal is worth noting to begin to appreciate what such an identification between gender history and Truth might mean. Essays by the then already leading feminist historians Gisela Bok and Alice Kessler-Harris set forth the stakes of US and international gender history. There was also an essay by Lydia Sklevicky on the origins, and suppression, of the field in Yugoslavia, grounded, appropriately, in an early twentieth-century journal dedicated to women and society, *Zenski svijet* (*Women's World*). We might be tempted to read Evelyn Brooks Higginbotham's contribution, "Beyond the Sound of Silence: Afro-American Women in History," as a rebuttal to or an indirect engagement with the cover image, though whether she knew Truth would be featured is unclear. What she wrote is that histories of Black women "call into question the concept of a universal womanhood by underscoring the unity of white men and

16

I Sell the Shadow to Support the Substance.

SOJOURNER TRUTH.

3. This image of the abolitionist Sojourner Truth is iconic in women's and African American history. It is similar to one that appeared on the front cover of the first issue of *Gender and History* in 1989, and it may have been one that Truth copyrighted and sold to fund her speaking tours.

women in determining American racial thought and policy. The white suffragists' vision of representative government excluded black women as well as black men." She followed this with the observation that while race was central to African American history, "gender and class preclude a monolithic black culture as well."

If we read Higginbotham's comments as a salvo, we can do so only in the limited context of *Gender and History*, since by 1989 her claims were standard fare, the articulation of a broad point of consensus in the African American women's history of the time. Together with the fact that the journal's editorial collective was transatlantic, Anglo-American, and by all accounts white (with respect to race and ethnicity, not unlike the profession at the time), it adds to the drama around the Sojourner Truth photograph and its positioning as the touchstone for the journal. Intentionally or not, through the combination of image and text, in this context and at this historical juncture, gender is made to serve as the prime signifier of a complex and unresolved set of social relations around race and sexuality in the field itself. *Gender and History,* for its part, serves as an archive of some of the earliest symptoms of the unruliness of those tensions in the profession.

The publication of *Gender and History* was undoubtedly a turning point for the field: a stake in the ground, but not the only one. For in keeping with the interrelatedness of these subjects in this period, the first issue of the *Journal of Women's History* also launched in 1989, and the *Journal of the History of Sexuality* premiered in 1990. And, of course, gender as a category of analysis has a long academic history, one that is linked as much to languages and linguistics and sociology and psychology as to history, if not more so. Robert Stoller's 1968 *Sex and Gender: The Development of Masculinity and Femininity* was among the first, and most influential, social scientific studies to map sex to biology and gender to culture—and to coin the phrase "gender identity."

In the 1970s gender became associated in feminist studies with social constructivism; its constructedness was embraced on the grounds that sexual and reproductive behaviors were "socially scripted" and therefore mutable, subject to adaptability and change in ways that hadn't been fully appreciated.

This constructivist turn was due in part to the influence of poststructuralism on Western critical thinking and to the impact of Michel Foucault's work in the social sciences. Without oversimplifying, we might say that Foucault's argument that "the subject must be attended to by 'creating a history of the different modes by which, in our culture, human beings are made subject'" resonated with feminist convictions not just about what gender is, but how gender is produced. There is no simple, let alone linear, explanation for the ascendancy of the sex/gender binarism in the conceptual lexicon of feminist critique. Indeed, much of the history of twentieth-century Western feminist theory revolves around the parsing, recasting, and undoing of the relay between sex/biology and gender/culture. In a recent attempt not so much to resolve as to dissolve the distinction between them, the feminist political theorist Samantha Frost offers a maxim that the gender historian may happily live with: "Biology and culture are patterns of activity that interpenetrate and work together differentially over time." We are, in other words, historically dynamic *biocultural* creatures.

If we cannot account for all the pathways through which practices of gender history first materialized between covers, we can identify a watershed moment in its early career: the publication of Joan Scott's "Gender: A Useful Category of Historical Analysis" in the academic journal of record for historians in the United States, the *American Historical Review* (*AHR*), in 1986—three years before the launch of *Gender and History*. In her article on the impact of Scott's landmark essay, Joanne Meyerowitz recalls that until its publication, gender history was a term rarely used. And only a handful of historians had examined men and masculinity as part of a *gender* history that did not focus solely on women. Scott was determined to insist on gender not simply as an identity attachable to masculinity or femininity, but as "a primary way of signifying relationships of power" and hierarchy in the terrain that is the past. Gender had the capacity to pry open subjects of history like the market or the state or war, she argued—arenas that appear to be unmarked by femininity or masculinity but in fact are constituted, produced even, through the ideological and material work of those categories. And gender itself is the effect, not the antecedent, of the work of history.

Armed with the logics of poststructuralism, Scott made a key distinction between gender as a dimension of identity and gender as an effect of operations in the terrain of power—rather than a self or a structure prior to it. Dorothy Ko helpfully calls this "the dual analytic edge of the category of gender—as social relationships and as power dynamics." With this analytical insight, Scott suggested how and why gender could reach well beyond the domain of men and women, transforming the discipline as a whole by denaturalizing the relationship between male and female and making all aspects of the past potentially available to a form of historical interpretation that was, effectively, resolutely feminist in orientation. And this insistence on gender as a category of analysis created a line in the sand between those who thought of gender as politicizing history and those who understand that gender history was a function of the politics of history itself.

For more than two decades, Scott's essay was the most downloaded of any *AHR* article on JSTOR. It was also reprinted in her 1988 collection of essays, *Gender and the Politics of History*, a title that became virtually synonymous with the field itself—and which, in the process, helped to popularize the "politics" (understood, à la Foucault, as dispersed vectors of power) of the practice more than any other work in gender history. But in Meyerowitz's assessment, its effects were ultimately mixed, at least in the context of US history. Scott came in for harsh criticism from many quarters, including accusations that she was erasing women as subjects from history and that the purchase of gender as a system of domination was weakened when gender was seen as difference per se. More tempered responses referenced work in fields like medieval history, where Caroline Walker Bynum's 1982 book *Jesus as Mother*, with its arguments about gendered inversion in the realm of spirituality, anticipated gender history— not least because medievalists had already started dissociating sex and gender.

Heidi Tinsman, for her part, represented US-based Latin American feminist historians with a characteristically thoughtful response in the *AHR* that politely refused a trickle-down theory from the West to the rest. She recalled how her own relationship to Scott's early work involved her in vigorous debates with Chilean scholars that mapped onto North-South colonial dynamics in instructive ways. Scott was certainly a lightning rod for critics who, whether feminists or not, were suspicious of French theory, and especially of what they perceived to be the threat of poststructuralism to the empirical basis of historical investigation. Whether her claims for gender history have been admired or scorned, they have cut deeply.

In fact, and despite the apparent success of Scott's arguments, both women's *and* gender history struggled to be recognized as legitimate fields well into the 1990s. And their practitioners fought to have their claims acknowledged as cogent and persuasive history. Books that are now considered defining events in the history of the field—such as Leonore Davidoff and Catherine Hall's monumental *Family Fortunes* (1987), which linked gender roles to industrial capitalism in Britain—were the subject of reviews that were as insulting as they were indifferent to the gender history therein. Interestingly, Davidoff and Hall engaged as much with women and men as they did with gender in their in-depth study of middle-class society in nineteenth-century Britain. They openly acknowledged their debt to feminist activism, and specifically to the women's liberation movement. They made a case for gender not as "an abstract logical grid," but, like class, as a material and symbolic force that was "worked out historically and...[that] emerged in social practices." And they self-consciously aimed to tell a "big" story about industrializing Britain that was built on evidence about gender and class, but which ramified to the national (if not the imperial) story.

Complaints were legion, from many quarters, but they ignored the book's contributions to gender history almost as often as they disparaged them. And in a review essay of nearly fifty pages that situated *Family Fortunes* in the historiography of both the gentry and the eighteenth century, Amanda Vickery called the history of separate spheres that Davidoff and Hall had been at pains to plot historically inaccurate—and in doing so scarcely touched on gender as a category of analysis in her lengthy, learned, and skeptical assessment. Even those who appreciated the argument could not resist a condescending sniff at the political presumptions behind *Family Fortunes*. In an otherwise serious and thoughtful assay of the book in the *Economic History Review* in 1988, the historian Harold Perkin concluded that, "however surprising it may be to modern feminists, most of these middle-class women...appeared to love their chains or at least to accept their dependent and supportive lot as the will of God. Feminist history may awaken our sympathy for the oppressed women of the past," he warned, "but it cannot alter their history or raise the consciousness of those dutifully dedicated and wilfully contented wives and mothers."

Davidoff and Hall were not acolytes of Scott. They had been researching and writing their book for at least ten years before it was published in 1987; their influences were British Marxism and its economic and sociological traditions rather than French theoretical work, and their massive tome is supported by deep empirical investigation, by example after example, and by a carefully plotted organizational structured designed to develop a gendered concept of class emerging from a distinctive socioeconomic milieu. As Hall observed in her introduction to the third edition of *Family Fortunes* in 2018 (Davidoff passed away in 2014), gender took a long time to emerge as a useful category of historical analysis. But the uncanny simultaneity of a provocation like Scott's essay and a monumental study like Davidoff and Hall's—not to mention the launching of *Gender and History*—signals how and why the 1980s was a watershed decade for the field. Significantly, Davidoff herself was the prime mover behind the establishment of *Gender and History*—a transatlantic collective that was predominantly white, UK-based, and determined to signal the "absolute distinctiveness" of its work.

Equally importantly, we find in Scott's argument about gender as "a primary way of signifying relationships of power" an antecedent of the trenchant yet ultimately qualified claim about the sovereignty of gender that we saw in the first *Gender and History* editorial. "A primary way" is such a fascinating choice of phrase, one that I have spent many hours parsing with students. "Primary" seems to stake one kind of claim; "a primary" seems to undermine it. Though she does gesture at race and class, Scott does not follow up with any specifics about what might complement or compete with gender as a useful category of analysis in her 1986 essay. Nor does she acknowledge the presumptively white and Western character of either her theoretical apparatus or the impact of those standpoints on her arguments for gender history as a global methodology.

Seen in this light, Scott's use of gender—as defined from modern Euro-American histories—assumes a de facto primacy, a universalism, that may matter as much, if not more so, than the words on the page. Tinsman offers a telling riff on this question when she writes of Scott's work that "it has never assumed the primacy that it did in North American debates about gender and subjectivity," and that Latin American feminist scholars had developed "a paradigm of our own."

It is hard to gainsay the impact of Scott's work on the development of gender history as an academic field. Love her or critique her, she put a big stake in the ground. Not all who grappled with gender derived their arguments from her, and not just those who worked beyond the West. If Scott came late to sexuality as a category of analysis, many scholars of the 1980s and 1990s understood women, gender, sexuality, and feminism as thoroughly entwined. Denise Riley put it well when she asked, "Does a sex have a history?" Her answer was that "any attention to the life of a woman, however it is traced in careful and elaborate description, must admit the degree to which the effects of gender are unpredictable and fleeting." And that

> the question of how far anyone can take on the identity of being a woman in a thoroughgoing manner recalls aspects of the "Active" status of sexual identities. Can anyone fully inhabit a gender without a degree of horror? How could someone "be a woman" through and through, make a final home in that category without suffering claustrophobia—or hysteria? To lead a life soaked in the passionate consciousness of one's gender at every moment, to will to be a sex with a vengeance—impossibilities, and far from the aims of feminism. Then what is it to be a woman sometimes?

Riley points to horizons not just beyond Scott but autonomous from her. Indeed, there were numerous, multisited conversations about the primacy of gender and of women in the project of dismantling (later, decolonizing) History with a capital H.

Two examples will suffice. The first is the work, in the 1980s, of the feminist postcolonial and poststructural literary critic Gayatri Spivak, who wrote two groundbreaking essays: "The Rani of Sirmur: An Essay in Reading the Archives" (published in *History and Theory* in 1985) and "Three Women's Texts and a Critique of Imperialism" (published in *Critical Inquiry* the same year). Each of these essays, differently but with the same unrelenting rhetorical force, challenges the sovereignty of gender over race or caste, reveals the presumptive whiteness of women in the very historical conception of feminism, and demands that European imperialism be rewritten into any and all accounts of modernity, gendered or not. The simultaneous publication of these blockbuster essays, which were to have an incalculable impact on the global history of gender well beyond the confines of one discipline, with the publication of Scott's *AHR* piece suggests how precarious even the qualified primacy of gender was as Scott was conscripting it.

The second example is the work of Elsa Barkley Brown, a professor in the Departments of History and Women's Studies at the University of Maryland, whose essay "Polyrhythms and Improvization: Lessons for Women's History" appeared in *History Workshop Journal* in 1991. Here she used the metaphors of jazz to argue for a relational understanding of difference. "Let me here grossly simplify," she wrote. "We have still to recognize that being a woman is, in fact, not extractable from the context in which one is a woman—race, class, time, and place. That is as true for white women as it is for African American, Latina, Asian, and Indian women. We have still to recognize that all women do not have the same gender. We cannot do that until we begin to put the experiences of the women we talk about in their relational context." Only then, she argued, can we "see all these conversations about where women's history has been and where it is going, about gender, about difference, about each of our own work … [and] be less entrenched in the need to defend our work, our takes on history, from all the people who want to rewrite the score."

What we now call intersectionality—a term coined by the legal scholar Kimberlé Crenshaw—was manifest in the deceptively simple claim that "all women do not have the same gender." The question for Brown was never the primacy but the relationality of difference at the site of race and ethnicity as well as gender. And for her, failure to recognize that relationality was troubling to all calls for change in the politics of history writing.

Spivak and Brown understood that gender history was emerging from a very specific set of locations—from inside the West and inside predominantly white communities—and was therefore not automatically or necessarily portable wholesale. It was not generalizable, not universal, as Higginbotham had put it. Histories of the whiteness of feminism as a movement and of feminist histories of women would soon take off, following on Angela Davis's early work *Women, Race and Class* (1981) and anticipating cries of "against white feminism" that were part of the many challenges to white power in the early 2020s.

As was evident from the first issues of *Gender and History* and the work of early practitioners, the instabilities and frictions of gender itself were part of the very vocation of the field. And it is important to reckon with those origins in order to understand the present. Simmering up from unequal conditions across the postwar world, they were also advance symptoms of social, economic, and political crises to come—as the Berlin Wall fell, Tiananmen Square was occupied, and the end of history was said to be nigh. Scholars grappling with what forms gender history could and should take inherited these tensions, and they shape the field down to the present.

# Chapter 2
# Gender history takes off

Gender history took root in academic writing in predominantly English-language publications after the 1980s. Grounded in a set of convictions that masculinity and femininity were constructed rather than found in nature, and that it was in social relations that the differences between them were made, this subfield of the discipline of history emerged against a backdrop of geopolitical crisis in which gender and gender history itself became part of the culture wars that remain with us today, both within and outside higher education. Though some of its practitioners sought to distinguish it from women's history, many scholars have thought of the two fields in tandem well into the twenty-first century. Meanwhile, the history of masculinity and the fields of queer and transgender history rose to prominence in this period, exhibiting kinships and affinities as well as differences of definition and method from gender history per se.

Seen in these contexts, it is possible to think of gender history as a matrix or a grid, a dense transfer point (to borrow from Foucault) for scholars interested in working out how power operates and, in turn, how best to historicize those operations across diverse times and places. The idea of gender as a matrix has shaped gender history since its formation in the 1980s, to such a degree that gender history itself may be said to be not simply a field but a *force* field, a site of critical energy and vibrant matter that has assembled and redistributed historical accounts of gender during an extended historical moment when its institutional legitimacy waxed and waned. What is the future of gender history? To discern this, we need to develop an understanding of its past.

Regardless of how wedded or indebted scholars who used it were to the arguments Joan Scott had laid out in the mid-1980s, the fact is that gender quickly took off as a category of historical analysis and cohered as a recognizable field in its own right. The fiction, shored up by the way that its name appears to give primacy to gender, is that the field has been exclusively focused on, say, characteristics of women or attributes of masculinity that are socially constructed. Work that posited both gender *in*

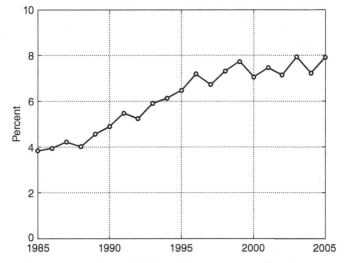

4. One way to measure the impact of historical scholarship on gender is to plot the rise and fall of work on the subject. This graph, which appeared in an article on abstracts in women's history by Sharon Block, suggests that 1985–2005 was a take-off period for women's history, overlapping with a similar acceleration in gender history. The percentage of history articles dealing with women rose from less than 4 percent in 1985 to about 8 percent in 2005.

and gender *as* history routinely grappled with how to assess when its centrality was warranted and, equally, how to right-size its historical role and its explanatory power in the making of histories at different scales. Histories of class, race, ethnicity, and indigeneity are some of the most obvious pressure points on gender as a unique expression of historical experience or change. So are age, ability, and other axes of identity and material life.

Historians have also run headlong into other forces, symbolic and material, that define how gender takes shape. They have had to account for culturally specific codes and customs of honor and conjugality and spirituality, for example, as they researched and taught how gender was made in a variety of national, regional, and local contexts. In so doing, they have toggled between gender as a dimension of identity and gender as the outcome of the collision of some bodies and selves with specific historical events or conditions. So we often read about the gendered nature of work in the Industrial Revolution, where women were assigned one form of labor, and men another. Or, where class is at issue, white and/or freed women were relegated to the home, and men to spaces like the office—resulting in the gendering of bourgeois public and private spheres. But we also read about the ways in which cataclysms like war or revolution, which throw women and men into radically new situations, generate new forms of gender identity—as when Western women were recruited to factory work in the First World War or when Russian women were recruited as settlers to the Soviet Far East under Stalin. In the latter two examples, we see the work of the state in actively innovating gender roles and redefining what counted as "womanly" in the process.

Hardly mutually exclusive, these approaches are nonetheless broadly characteristic of gender history in practice down to the present. And it is rare enough that proof of gender's analytical and historical power does not involve considerable engagement with women and men, racialized masculinities and class-based femininities, not to mention the full range of fluid possibilities. Gender history and the history of sexuality converged and diverged, though they were often extremely interdependent. Meanwhile, if gender history is shorthand for a diversity of methods and subjects, it is also a metonym for the politics of all history. Indeed, in its most prolific and influential forms, gender history has been a carrier of modes of narrating both the past of gender and its entanglement with more than one axis of identity, meaning, and, above all, power.

In 1986 Leila Ahmed opened her essay on "Women and the Advent of Islam" by suggesting that Aisha rather than Khadija should be considered the first woman of Islam. She reasoned that Khadija, "the wealthy widow who employed Mohamad to oversee her caravan (trading between Mecca and Syria) and proposed to and married him when she was forty and he twenty-five, was already in her fifties when Mohamad received his first revelation and began to preach Islam." Aisha, on the other hand, was born to Muslim parents and was betrothed to Muhammad when she was a child and he had already begun his career—so that it was Aisha's life that would "foreshadow changes that Islam would effect for women in Arabia." What follows is a brilliant exposition of the impact of matrilineal and patrilineal systems on the origins of Islamic tradition, helping to explain how the Prophet's marriages reflected the ways that Islam consolidated changes already under way in Arabia. Women's identities as wives, traders, and religious authorities hold the key to the origins of the dramatic social change that Islam brought to the region and the wider world.

In 1992 Ahmed published her book *Women and Gender in Islam: Historical Roots of a Modern Debate*, which opened with an apologia for taking up women and gender together, on the grounds that Western apprehensions about Muslim women were inaccurate. Such misunderstandings required a critical survey of discourses about women *and* gender as a way of redressing inaccuracies—"whether in the popular media or the academy...[about] the merits or demerits of Islam or Arab culture—about the history of women and Islam. The investigation of the discourses on women and gender in Islamic Middle Eastern societies entails studying the societies in which they are rooted, and in particular the way in which gender is articulated socially, institutionally, and verbally in these societies," Ahmed argued. "Unearthing and piecing together the history of women and the articulation of gender in Muslim societies, areas of history largely invisible in Middle Eastern scholarship, thus was a...major part of this enterprise." And she reprinted "Women and the Advent of Islam" as chapter 4 of the book.

This example underscores how thoroughly gender history was connected to, and indeed dependent on, women's history well after *Gender and History* declared itself a professional domain. It also indicates how closely geopolitics shadowed scholarship in the field: to make her point about women and gender, Ahmed invoked the "clash of civilizations" debate that would so heavily inform responses to 9/11, the war on terror, and the American debacle in Afghanistan.

The 1990s witnessed a veritable explosion of research and publication that modeled what gender history looked like across any number of fields. The emphasis was typically on gender relations and dominant gender ideologies, as in Clare Midgley's 1992 *Women against Slavery: The British Campaigns, 1780–1870*, which operated from the presumption that "gender divisions and roles structured the organization, activities, ideologies and policies" of the abolitionist movement in ways that were consequential to its outcomes and had not previously been acknowledged or fully understood. Midgley posited that, alongside class, gender was key to the intersection of industrial capitalism and slavery as a system—and also that she was not simply interested in adding women to the mix. Her study was inspired by Joan Scott's determination to analyze the ways in which "politics construct gender and gender constructs politics." Studies like

Midgley's mapped gender and race onto social histories even as they sought to distinguish analysis of gender history from the story of women per se.

In Midgley's case, as elsewhere, this was partly because of the way that social historians had begun to catch women up on the way to other topics—philanthropy, slavery, capitalism itself—without bringing sufficient weight to bear on analytics like gender ideology or the work of difference in constituting the social relations at hand. Midgley, for her part, not only viewed masculinity as a significant domain of gender. She also wove it into her analysis of how abolition politics worked, acknowledging the ways that "the supposedly gender-neutral concept of the brotherhood of man" shaped abolitionist claims, as with the "Am I not a Man and a Brother" meme that circulated so widely as part of antislavery campaigns in Britain.

Taking aim at historical subjects traditionally unmarked by gender, historians began to reshape the terrain upon which they grasped everything from politics to revolution, from science to war. There are some notable examples from the late twentieth century of how boldly historians embraced gender as a causal agent in history. Kristin Hoganson's *Fighting for American Manhood*, subtitled *How Gender Politics Provoked the Spanish-American and Philippine-American Wars*, advanced the argument that "the political pressure to assume a manly posture and appear to espouse manly policies gave gender beliefs the power to affect political decision-making" and even provided the impetus to war at the turn of the century. Londa Schiebinger's *Nature's Body: Gender and the Making of Modern Science* was equally direct:

> Beginning in my doctoral dissertation, I identified three analytically distinct but interlocking pieces of the puzzle: the story of women themselves and the history of their participation in science, the history and structure of scientific institutions as mediators between science as a body of knowledge and society, and questions of how

regimes of gender have molded the results of science.... [M]y purpose in *Nature's Body* was to go beyond an analysis of women's bodies (those skeletons in the closet of science) to look specifically at the third aspect of my analytic triad, namely, how science is not value neutral but participates in and continues to support human knowledge that is highly gendered.

Schiebinger's work showed the capacity of gender as a historical force and even as a regime of power to shape scientific knowledge and to make history. And she left little doubt as to the strength of her conviction on these points when she declared, "I take it to be the point of the history of science and the history of gender to show that neither science nor transhistorical bodies exist apart from culture."

Historiography on the French Revolution is an especially rich site for gauging how these reconsiderations worked in practice, as scholars gravitated toward the events of 1789 and after to test theories of how gender operated and how gender identities were made and unmade in the turmoil of political upheaval. Using the vast repertoire of texts and visual imagery generated by republicans and opponents alike, Joan Landes, a feminist historian of the revolutionary years, emphasized "the power of gendered imagery in helping (negatively) to destroy the icons and symbols of Old Regime state and society and (affirmatively) to create a new citizen body within a republican nation state." In the process, she consolidated the argument that gender participated in the process whereby subjects became citizens—and with it, the idea that revolution was itself a field of "gender possibility."

The links between women and gender history have remained tight in this subfield of French history. In *Fabricating Women*, her monumental 2001 study of French seamstresses in the lead-up to 1791, Clare Crowston set out to investigate the effects of gender on women's work in the trades. Using gender to refer to culturally and socially constructed notions of sexual difference, she contends that precisely with the growth of women's access to guild privileges, *"couturière* acquired stricter professional and gender connotations." Crowston and others rejected the notion that politics or labor before or during the Age of Revolution was an exclusively male domain. Feminist historians began to question this emphasis on political exclusion and domestication as the primary impact of the French Revolution on women, and to see the question of gender and citizenship as a lens through which to examine a variety of trends in the making of modern France.

In the context of Haiti and other French colonial spaces, gender identity could be intersected by dynamics of race on the ground, meaning that family and marriage as sites of race and creolization were key to the operations of power in a state such as Saint-Domingue after 1793. As it turns out, both French republicans and Haitian rebels like Toussaint L'Ouverture shared a set of convictions about how marriage among former slaves could and should stabilize the moral order and sustain the sexual division of work needed for the coercive labor regimes of the mid-to-late 1790s to prosper. In 1793, for example, an enslaved man could achieve emancipation and hence a degree of manhood by joining the French Revolutionary army. But an enslaved woman had to marry to win her freedom. Significantly, some female slaves married recently freed men to win emancipation. In any case, in France and Haiti, as well as in countless other times and places, if and when family served as a productive space for contesting or reshaping gender relations, such possibilities were typically highly contingent on when and where family formation took place. And, in mid-revolution, they were likely to prove fleeting to boot.

What of historical geographies beyond the West, if not beyond empire and colonialism? Histories of women and gender and revolution were certainly not limited to Europe—and like revolutions themselves, they have been in a constant state of flux and reimagination. Gail Hershatter, one of the leading historians of gender and the Chinese Revolution writing in the West, argued that what made gender radical, in the sense of disorderly, was not its capacity to push the space of the political past the realm of protest and regime change, or even to help us see power at multiple scales: family community, village, nation. Resisting the tendency to over-claim for gender as a central lens or optic, she suggests we understand, and use it, as "an anchoring, a foothold." From this vantage point we can appreciate that it "is not always the self-same thing wherever it is found." This sounds like an uncanny echo of Elsa Barkley Brown's observation that "we have still to recognize that all women do not have the same gender."

For US-based historians of Latin America in the lead-up to the new millennium, the entanglement of gender and honor emerged as key to understanding how women were linked both to moral and social order and to how politics operated in real and symbolic terms. Here, the mobilization of gender was in answer to very specific historiographical trends. As Sarah Chambers wrote in *From Subjects to Citizens* (1999), "that the discourse of republican honor was masculine indicates that gender was central to [the] political transition [in eighteenth- and nineteenth-century Peru]." Despite the explosion of work in Latin American women's history, she lamented that most interpretations ignored gender. "Although women were ultimately marginalized within the political sphere," she argued, "the ideologically defined boundary between public and private space was more porous in practice." That is, because republican authorities needed men to service war and the economy, they were willing to shore up the power of the men in the private sphere, with profound consequences for women's lives. Among these consequences was an emphasis on female virtue as private morality, which in Latin America as elsewhere justified the exclusion of women from politics and allowed officials to regulate female sexuality on the grounds that it was key to social order.

For a different time and place—Brazil in the twentieth century—Sueann Caufield made a series of arguments about gender and honor in *In Defense of Honor* (2000). For Latin American elites, "sexual honor stood for a set of gender norms that, with their apparent basis in nature, provided the basis for unequal power relations in public and private life." Sexual honor was invoked to reinforce hierarchical relations based not only on gender, but on race and class as well. In these claims we hear evidence of how gender operated as a material force in a field of power and as a dimension of identity, exerting influence in public and private as well as in liminal spaces—like urban centers—in between. Also audible is the crosshatching of class and race and sexuality as interlocking domains that fortify gender's historical impact, most often at the expense of women.

In African history, scholars of gender in the 1980s went up against a powerful paradigm—the nationalist narrative—whose capacity to flatten the complexity of anticolonial struggle was not easily challenged. As Megan Vaughan noted, a terminological problem from the colonial period became a historiographical and methodological one for the field of gender history. "The problem of women," she suggested, "was shorthand for a number of related problems including changes in property rights, in rights in labour and relations between generations" (cited in Jean Allman's "Rounding Up Spinsters"). The real issue was that convulsive changes taking place in economic relations put enormous pressure on gender relations—changes attributed to negative stereotypes like degeneration, sexual promiscuity, and disease. In her work on colonial Asante, Jean Allman explored this very pattern in service of what she called "a gendered periodization of the development of the cocoa economy"—a chronology that helped explain why political upheaval was seen as a crisis in morality and sexuality in the interwar period. Allman, Susan Geiger, Claire Robertson, and Teresa Barnes are all among the first generation of historians working in the Western academy to think through gender and, in the case of Barnes especially, "to demonstrate the salience of gendered history to an improved understanding of the urban past"—in her case, in Zimbabwe. Barnes's 1999 study, *We Women Worked So Hard,* was hailed as an innovative approach to gender through an emphasis on social reproduction—the latter best described as a multilayered process at the intersection of gender and social power.

As one reviewer of Barnes's book commented, "within African Women's Studies, much discussion has centered on whether Western gender categories are valid at all for African women. Many scholars now recognize that the term gender is 'slippery' and 'situational,' while remaining essential to any analysis of people's lives." In contrast, Barnes's research was carefully grounded in African women's words and perspectives, thanks to the extensive oral history that undergirded her narrative. Widely praised for the nuance it brought to previous work on colonial gender relations, Barnes followed the evidence of the gendered character of Zimbabwean political economy by demonstrating that it was not the state that exerted control over African women; rather, some African males developed new notions of female decency and respectability, which impacted women's mobility. Barnes identified what she called "marital migrancy," where "wives seeking to live with urban-dwelling husbands, and to gain greater access to commodities, remained free from the taint of urban life by keeping a foot in the 'old' world of rural reproduction."

Of note is the way Barnes shows how gender relations were woven into and through the broader political history of Harare. As the reviewer also noted, "she explains the notorious rape of elite female hostel dwellers during the bus boycott of 1956 in terms of both the challenge their independent status offered to male notions of patriarchy, and their relatively higher class position over poor men." If *"We Women Worked So Hard"* remains a staple of African social history syllabi even now, it's because it opened the door to a rewriting of urban, gender, and nationalist histories all at once. And if there was any doubt that histories of women, gender, and sexuality were entwined with those of race and class, studies like this one modeled how and why in enduring ways.

In a 1993 survey of new work in African women's and gender history, Paul Zeleza insisted that "the tendency to talk indiscriminately of 'African men' must be resisted, for African men, no less than African women, were not homogeneous. They differentiated according to class, status, and occupation, so that they did not share similar interests with regards to women's position in society." Within the next decade, histories of masculinity across the continent would more than keep pace with African women's history. Colonialism was held responsible for creating new forms of masculine identity, transforming them through histories of race and class—and, in Southern Africa, with making the language of white men and "black 'boys'" a standard part of the lexicon.

As histories of men and masculinity in Africa took off, subjects ranged from the making of manhood in Christianity and Islam, to labor regimes and worker militancy and their impact on and for gender, to the making of nationalist and vernacular forms at times of crisis and in everyday life. Masculinity functioned here as a relational category as well as an intersectional one, where "intersectional" might refer to tribal or ethnolinguistic norms as well as racial identity per se. Tracking negotiations of masculinity in his 2005 *Making Men in Ghana*, Stephan Miescher emphasized the pull of community culture as well as of missionary and other colonial models. And while he acknowledged the significance of such history for women's and gender history, he also suggested what an instructive foil it could be, especially over the course of a century of change.

Nancy Cott observed in her address to the American Historical Association's annual meeting in 2005 that "gender history not only recognizes women as historical agents but also revokes the assumption that men are neuter beings whose masculinity and sexuality require no notice." If these subjects were prominent from the start, they were also often considered to be key to the fullest understanding of the politics of women's history. One of the earliest advocates of gender-as-masculinity history, John Tosh, was keen to historicize ideologies of masculinity and the various codes by which it was expressed for their own sake, and also because of the ways they operated "at the expense of women." Kathleen Brown, in her 1996 study *Good Wives, Nasty Wenches, and Anxious Patriarchs*, insisted that attention to a man's plural and dispersed power "as husband, father, master, and head of household in colonial Virginia" was key to understanding everything from women's subordination to "Indian virility" in the early republic.

Indeed, some of the most important early work on men and masculinities was done by early modernists whose interdisciplinary research and reading practices made them alive to the malleability of gender roles before modernity hardened them. Scholars working before, say, 1800 were also keenly aware of how premodern gender systems, such as the complementary ones that characterized Andean polities, could influence the consolidation of Spanish rule. This insistence on gender's history in deep time led Merry Wiesner-Hanks, a true doyenne of gender histories of the early modern world, to make a case for "gendered temporalities" that, while keyed to women's gendered experiences, are nonetheless inclusive of masculinity and the evidence of the historical processes so indispensable to the making of norms about manhood.

The journal *Gender and History* had spotlighted the subject of masculinity in its first two issues, featuring research articles on early modern guilds and male workers in three different settings. Though femininity and indeed Western histories of gender tended to predominate in the first decade or so of the journal, articles on men and masculinities frequently shaped the table of contents. Among those was my own essay, on Behramji Malabari, a nineteenth-century Indian social reformer whose perambulations I tracked from Bombay to London, in an effort to show that "performances of masculinity can be strategically mobilized according to specific, situational asymmetries of power, and that men subordinated by hegemonic gender norms are capable of deploying other forms of masculinity both to resist domination and to create subordinates of their own." This research was consonant with other projects in the field of imperial history invested in calling out the links between masculine gender codes and the sexual identity of colonizer and colonized—as in the work of Mrinalini Sinha, which aimed to show that masculinity never operated outside colonial power structures, and that the conditions and crises of imperial rule were equally dependent on stereotypes of women, with economic and legal consequences for patriarchal politics.

Given the Western liberal progressive narrative of women first, gender second—and of whites first, Blacks second—it is important to note that those in the first post-1970s generation of African American historians had histories of race and masculinity squarely in their sights. Darlene Clark Hine and Earnestine Jenkins's 1999 reader, *Manhood Rights*, was a powerful collection whose introductory chapter, "Black Men's History: Toward a Gendered Perspective," made the stakes of materializing "ancestral black male legacies" and "black male culture" indubitably clear. They were not shy about situating their work in the context of contemporary US crises, giving leading Black sociologist Aldon D. Morris the lead in the preface to their book. "The editors of this volume," he wrote,

> are well aware that the negative male image is the one most often associated with African American men. Indeed, the popular imagination, the media, and social science literature have focused on the Black male as criminal, violent, family deserter, lazy and shiftless predator, and extremely self-centered.... In short, African American males emerge from these venues as dangerous, menacing, and a drain on the resources of the larger society. Their rates of incarceration and homicide appear to confirm the validity of the negative Black male image.

In their view, "academia has been obsessed with portraying Black men as a sociological ill."

Hine and Jenkins prefaced their reader with a call to examine the history of Black men from a gendered perspective in order to facilitate the ongoing project of reconstructing American history. Even the most casual observer of the first two decades of gender history research will be struck by the way that concerns about masculinity as a necessary component of gender surfaced, both in essays dedicated to the subject and in projects more focused on gender-as-women. When Scott McCracken spoke about the rise of a "gender industry" in the profession, he could do so confident in the knowledge that gender history was not the exclusive purview of scholars interested in femininity, let alone scholars who identified as women.

If gender history was to be the story of how femininity and masculinity operated, and how women and men were made, in the past, it was also indispensable, as a field, to understandings of how sexual difference and sexuality itself were to be read as articulations emerging from specific times and places. Joan Scott famously moved her attention from gender to sexual difference as the defining category. Joanne Meyerowitz summarizes this reorientation nicely. In the 1980s Scott had argued that gender had "seemed a useful category of analysis precisely because it had an unfamiliar, destabilizing effect." By 1999, however, Scott felt that it had "lost its ability to startle and provoke." Gender had all too quickly, and lamentably, become "a synonym for women, for the differences between the sexes, for sex."

Even allowing for the tremendous influence of Scott's work, a reading of the field of gender history in its first two decades suggests that this move is less a turning point than a sign of entanglement of sexuality and gender in history from the start. For one thing, sexuality and its histories were always entailed in the history of gender, and the field in turn sponsored conversations and debates about sexual attitudes and concepts, rape and other forms of sexual coercion, sexuality and conjugality, sex work, and more. Of all the studies we might cite, Laura Engelstein's 1992 history of prostitution in Russia, *The Keys to Happiness: Sex and the Search for Modernity in Fin-de-Siècle Russia*, made it indubitably clear that sexual deviance and gender roles were intertwined, in this case shaping the terms upon which "fallen women" became juridical subjects of the law, the site of sexual regulation of gender identities.

Not all historians have read sexuality and gender through deviance. And when they have, they have been keen to show how deviance is also not simply to be found in nature or in history, but is rather an effect of gender politics itself. This insight was among the signal contributions of Judith Walkowitz's influential 1980 study, *Prostitution and Victorian Society*, which tracked how class and gender prerogatives shaped male anxieties about streetwalkers—with fatal consequences for many of them. For other historians, the path of historicizing relationships between sexuality and gender runs through desire. Pete Sigal's work, first on Mayan culture and then on Nahua ritual, is exemplary for its ability to hold histories of gender, sexuality, and colonial culture in productive tension. And in her sweeping history of desire in the West, Anna Clark shows how it is possible to see individuals and institutions using the regulation of sexual desires and behaviors to "control the boundaries of gender" at scale—that is, in broad patterns that are visible over hundreds of years.

The *Journal of the History of Sexuality*, founded in 1990, quickly became an important outlet for work focused expressly on these subjects. Gender historians continued to explore histories of sexuality whenever they addressed gender as a socially constructed system embedded in material and symbolic conditions as lived by "men" and "women." This was as true for Leila Ahmed's treatment of women and the advent of Islam as it was for Kathleen Brown's study of colonial Virginia or Mrinalini

Sinha's account of colonial masculinity and "Bengal effeminacy," not least because all of these histories are concerned with the entanglement of social and sexual reproduction. As Scott herself noted in 2008, gender as an "analytic tool" need not be "a substitute for women's history." Likewise, you need a history of gender(s) in order to grasp how modes of sexualization come to make men and women in historically contingent and dynamic ways. And to figure out, as Denise Riley had asked around the time Scott's 1986 essay appeared, what it might "mean to be a woman sometimes."

Exactly how, why, and under what conditions such modes of being gendered manifested is not the story of gender history alone, but of queer and transgender history as well. In their 2012 state-of-the-field essay, Cornelia Dayton and Lisa Levenstein wrote that in the United States, women's and gender history have functioned together as a big tent, with practitioners positioning themselves at the intersection of several fields—even as they might all agree that the work of overcoming resistance to integrating this work into the discipline as a whole is ongoing. This is not to say there have not been disagreements about evidence, sharp debates about interpretation, or divergences over method and politics within the field. How has the field as constituted held up or shifted in the last decade? The gender binary at the heart of the origins of gender history has been prized open, not only by the work of queer history, but also by the emergence of the body as a right and proper historical subject, and, above all, by the ways in which engagements with histories outside the West compel the realization that gender, binary or not, is always already an effect of the geopolitics of time and place.

As Kevin Murphy and Jennifer Spear noted in 2010, "new work in the field of transgender studies has shown that subsuming categories of gender difference within an analysis of sexuality is problematic because it figures a western conception of homosexuality as normative." Having a sense of gender history's beginnings and its early decades is key for discerning its future. Examining the conundrum at the heart of gender as a "primary" category of analysis and/or history is something we must reckon with in order to appreciate what the limits and possibilities of gender history have come to be, particularly as we consider the historical conditions that produce that future.

# Chapter 3

# Intersectionality and the making of gender history

If the primacy or singularity of gender as a category of historical analysis has been in question since the formal beginnings of gender history as a field, the story of its intersection with other categories involved in the making of history is not necessarily well known. Or, where that story is available, it is often informally cast as a tale of progressive enlightenment in which gender history struggles to free itself from the vise of Marxist attachments to class, bursts forth on the scene as the vehicle for new forms of social and cultural history, followed by the "discovery" and application of race in a similar vein, followed by queer and transgender histories as the logical denouement of our present.

Such a narrative may have had some legitimacy in some fields. But attachment to it as a grand narrative underplays the opposition to gender history many scholars in the first generation experienced in response to their written work and, in ways harder to document, the resistance they faced both in the job market and in other less public venues to their commitment to challenge the objectivity of history as a discipline. It also runs the danger of overlooking how indifferent some of the most well-known historians of the late twentieth century were to it, especially (though not only) at its beginnings, taking little or no notice of gender as indispensable to the way we understand major events and epochs. So while Nell Irvin Painter acknowledged that Eric

Foner's *Reconstruction: America's Unfinished Revolution* (1988) was clearly a monumental accomplishment, she also pointedly objected to the fact that he neglected the ways that gender, sex, and marriage shaped Reconstruction politics.

Inside the field of gender history itself, there have been heated debates as well. Some have worried about the abstractions of gender producing disembodied histories of women and men. Others express concern over whether a focus on gender deflected attention from feminist history and its emancipatory ambitions. But these are not the only frictions below the surface of any would-be progressive telling of the story of gender history. For gender and class continued to be bound up well beyond the first outcroppings of the field itself. And attention to race as both a material structure and an identity category hardly followed behind but was entailed, at least in some quarters, from the beginning of academic conversations about gender history, most notably in its flagship journal.

Even allowing for their quarrels with both the kinds of gender and the kinds of sexuality presumed to constitute gender history as a practice, queer and trans histories have not been latecomers to the heyday (if there was one) of gender history. Nor can they be seen perforce as an improvement on it. As "a primary" way of signifying power, gender has provided one of the key methods for historicizing everything from revolution to everyday life, relying on binary ways of thinking, challenging them, and, above all, seeking to capture the historical dynamism of gender whatever expression it has taken. Key to any account of gender history, then, is the story of who embraced what came to be called "intersectionality," how they have positioned gender in that framework, and how gender has positioned them.

As is well known, intersectionality came into the US scholarly lexicon through the work of the African American legal scholar Kimberlé Crenshaw. She coined the concept in a 1989 article (the year *Gender and History* was founded) in order to invoke the costs to Black women when "dominant conceptions of discrimination condition us to think about subordination as disadvantage occurring along a single categorical axis." Drawing on a combination of African women's history, legal scholarship, and the Civil Rights Act of 1964 itself, she set out to show "that Black women are sometimes excluded from feminist theory and antiracist policy discourse because both are predicated on a discrete set of experiences that often does not accurately reflect the interaction of race and gender." This groundbreaking essay (published in the *University of Chicago Legal Forum*) has since been summarized, glossed, and pathologized. It has become, and remains, one of the bedrocks of critical race theory by any name.

Beyond its rootedness in civil rights law, Crenshaw's argument grew out of a number of court cases, including one involving General Motors, which drew a direct line between discriminatory workplace treatment and the social and political crises brought on by African Americans' quest for citizenship and equality before the law. She cited Daniel Moynihan's "diagnosis" of the "ills of Black society" in his infamous 1965 report on the Black family, as well as the controversy over the 1985 movie *The Color Purple*, to underscore the short- and long-term contexts in which ignorance of the compounded nature of discrimination as an intersectional practice operated at an unacceptable cost to Black individuals and communities. Crenshaw minced no words about the link between contemporary racial injustice inside and outside the courtroom and the history of Black women and feminism from Sojourner Truth forward.

When it comes to how they conceptualized their categories, the epistemological kinship between Kimberlé Crenshaw and Joan Scott is striking. Scott argued for gender not as a historical phenomenon but as an effect of historical forces in a field of power. Crenshaw's emphasis on an "understanding of how crosscutting forces establish gender norms" speaks to a similar conviction that gender is not found in but produced through history. Contemporary Black scholars took a similar view of race in the Anglophone context. In the well-known formulation of Black British cultural theorist Stuart Hall, race was not fixed, but was produced as a result of the pressures of historical time and place; it was a "floating signifier." Nor was it singular. For Hall, class was the modality in which race was lived—an observation that led Paul Gilroy to suggest that gender was the modality in which race was lived. How did scholars invested in gender history track the lived realities of this compound relationship, these intersectional modes of being and belonging, of making cultural life, of doing and undoing politics, war, revolution, family, labor, freedom?

Many of the discussions and debates around gender's right and proper relationship to race as an axis of intersectionality played themselves out in the pages of academic journals in the 1990s and beyond. As Eileen Boris argued in the *Journal of Women's History* (*JWH*) in 1994, "'race' has been the undertheorized category of the analytic trinity of gender, 'race,' and class; it is too often taken as natural rather than socially, culturally, and politically constructed. For too many, 'race' still appears to exist in the realm of the biological rather than being seen, like gender, as an identity that is created."

Less than a decade later in that same venue, Rosalind Rosenberg made a case for the "conjunction" of race and gender in her examination of the works of Pauli Murray. Using the idiom of "Jane Crow," Rosenberg showed that Murray herself had argued that "arbitrary classifications of race...worked in 'conjunction' with arbitrary classifications of gender to create particularly oppressive conditions for minority women." Yet, Rosenberg contended, "in most discussions about gender and race, black women disappeared. Discrimination was treated either as a problem faced by black men or, by analogy, as an obstacle confronted by white women. Rarely was it analyzed as a burden that fell with particular force upon minority women." The *JWH* was committed, in other words, to interrogating gender, out of a sense that "axes of power other than gender often exercise a critical role in the shaping of women's lives." And it supported work which offered evidence of the ways that the work of gender could be subordinated to or muted by the historical force of class or race, whether as systems of power and/or as sites of struggle.

*Gender and History* continued to be a critical venue for staging conversations about the ethical and political commitments of gender history and gender historians, with Michele Mitchell, a member of the journal's collective, at the forefront of these questions. In the introduction to one such issue in 1999, Mitchell reminded readers that African American women's history had been well on its way to establishing itself when *Gender and History* began, and that "African Americanist gender history has consistently noted how specific phenomena—subjugation, racist discourse, attempts to realize collective improvement, initiatives for community mobilization, longings for self-determination, desires to break free from social strictures—spurred black women and men to seize or alter mainstream gender conventions." Though not especially commonly employed, Mitchell's use of the phrase "African Americanist gender history" nonetheless signals the ways in which entanglements of race and gender marked the first twenty years of *Gender and History*'s existence, albeit in a context heavily influenced by US racial history and Black experience.

In contrast, Indigenous histories of women and gender did not fare as well in the early days of *Gender and History*, where title searches for "Native" American and Indigenous turn up little before the 2010s. Where the term "Native" comes up, it is typically in relation to history outside the US context, though mainly as a descriptive and not as an analytical category. We need only consider the careers of Ojibwe historian Brenda Child and Hawaiian anthropologist J. Kehaulani Kauanui, for whom the politics of gender and family and gender and decolonization have long been central, or to look beyond the earliest issues of women's and gender history journals to see what venues scholars choose for this work—work that is often intersectional at the site of race and gender. That research on gender and Native history is not to be found in anything like a critical mass in *Gender and History* raises important questions about who gained ground and why in this signature space for the field. Indigenous archival erasure is as much if not more of a burden for gender history as for the discipline at large. Ironically, as Tadashi Dozono reminds us, "learning about different ways of making sense of gender, particularly Indigenous gender systems, makes for good historical thinking," not least because it takes aim at universals, grounding gender binaries in specificities of time and place.

Journals were critical for bringing new work to the fore because they signaled that the field was institutionalized like any other. But it is only by thinking through the landmark books published during the period 1985–2015 that we can fully appreciate how and why intersectional approaches became so critical to what gender history was to become. What follows is not a definitive list but rather a modest attempt to read for intersectional approaches that have grappled with how to do more than add gender, how to do more than see race, how to think across multiple categories of analysis and axes of identity—how to historicize, in short, evidence of the work of intersectionality as it shaped the past. I've approached this through a set of thematic groupings, not for their representativeness but as a strategy for discerning patterns and pairings. We can think of it as a kind of syllabus for the history of gender history.

Let us start with histories of Atlantic world slavery, which have been transformed not just by women's or gender history but also by the determination of scholars, Black and Brown and white, to "analyze race and gender in tandem"—and, of course, to think about labor, reproduction, and sexuality through that binocular vision. Deborah Gray White's *Ar'n't I a Woman?: Female Slaves in the Plantation South* (1985) was pioneering precisely because it was the first study to attend comprehensively to such subjects, particularly at the scale of the everyday. It is remarkable how intersectionality, though at that time still unnamed, shaped every aspect of White's investigation. Simply put: "Black in a white society, slave in a free society, woman in a society ruled by men, female slaves had the least formal power and were, perhaps, the most vulnerable group of antebellum Americans." White acknowledged the challenges of the archive, especially when it came to the private worlds of enslaved women, challenges that those who came after her have continued to grapple with in highly inventive and methodologically original ways.

Gender was key to White's analysis, though she used it selectively—in reference, for example, to the organization of plantation labor regimes ("gender must have provided a natural and easy way to divide the labor force") and to the particular idioms of white southern womanhood (middle-class white women "retreated to the race-grounded gender ideology that required them to hide their personal strength under a veil of femininity in order to claim the 'ladydom' that was the privilege of whiteness"). Nor did gender protect Black women from white terror, as the many examples of brutal beatings, rapes, and murders that White elucidates as part of her evocation of the fabric of daily life under slavery powerfully testify. For White, in short, there was no doubt that race and gender together shaped the life cycle of the female slave: "[R]ace, class, gender, sexuality, and other identity variables do not exist independently. Nor do they compete for supremacy, but reinforce, overlap, and intersect each other."

The significance of White's work for bringing race and gender to the fore through the story of enslaved women cannot be underestimated. It was widely reviewed both in and outside of professional journals (the *LA Review of Books* called it a "fusillade" and "engrossing"). It sold 200,000 copies in the first twenty years and was deemed worthy of a place in the canon next to W. E. B. Du Bois's

*The Souls of Black Folk.* Thanks not only to her scholarship but also to her teaching and mentoring, several generations of Black women historians are as indebted to White herself as they are to *Ar'n't I a Woman*, building out as they have from her book and taking intersectional approaches to enslavement in new directions.

One such study is Jennifer Morgan's 2004 *Laboring Women*, whose subtitle, *Reproduction and Gender in New World Slavery*, points to the nexus of race and gender at the site of labor and capital and, as she says at the start of the book, to the impossibility of historicizing women or gender in ways "unmodified by race." Morgan's research comes out of archives in both South Carolina and Barbados, in part to help us appreciate how easily the compounding of racial and gender ideologies traveled across colonial spaces before the nineteenth century, and that indeed it was that very compound logic which animated calculations about European profit and prosperity. Here the stakes of reproduction are at once social and sexual: "[T]o write the history of racial ideology without gender," she argues, "is to omit the most fundamental reality of race as a trope—its heritability." Upon laboring women, and upon their raced and gendered value as mothers in particular, rested nothing less than the reproductive futurity of the plantation complex itself.

Like White, Morgan's archives are unyielding of the kinds of historical knowledge that might give a fuller context to the names of enslaved women gleanable from planters' wills and other soulless empirical data. Though "critical fabulation" is a 2020s term made available by the work of Saidiya Hartman and others, in *Laboring Women*, Morgan anticipated it in her determination to speculate responsibly about how enslaved mothers may have reasoned and even felt. She balanced standards of historical evidence with the imperative to compensate for literal erasure. Marisa Fuentes's *Dispossessed Lives: Enslaved Women, Violence, and the Archive* (2018) exemplifies how to confront such archival limits through strategically inventive interpretation. Here the intersection of histories of race, gender, and sexuality together compel a confrontation not simply with the absences of the official record or even its evidence of brutality and terror. The archives of enslavement and emancipation become a site where the multiple burdens of dispossession are reenacted—and produce, for Fuentes, a call to "read against the bias grain." Like the informal market economy, where some enslaved and free women might be said to have enjoyed moments of autonomy, the archive has "reproduced colonial power and reinforced social, racial and gendered hierarchies."

For Fuentes, as for Morgan and White before her, a variety of labor regimes—with their disciplining capacity and their links to the accumulation and reproduction of capital—are key to the racial and gendered codes emerging from fields of power like the marketplace, and redeploying them as well. And, as with Morgan, Fuentes pushes back against archival erasure, opening each chapter with vignettes that build up and out from archival fragments in creative ways. Though there are many explanations for this particular genre of archival critique in the history of Atlantic world slavery, the pursuit of how, why, and under what conditions race and gender work together may be said to have contributed to new ways of bringing history "into a more transparent and reflexive frame."

Because of histories of enslavement in the United States and the crisis of US politics around race in the 1980s and 1990s (the killing of Vincent Chin; the riots in Crown Heights, Brooklyn, and Los Angeles) and after, intersectionality was a key component in US gender history perhaps as nowhere else. Textbooks designed for survey courses in American history were an important site for the representation of that much cited triumvirate: class, race, and gender. To the extent that sexuality was evident from the start, it came increasingly into view as historians strove to remake the US past with an eye to examining and debating the "created equal" credo in high school and university classrooms. Among the most important and influential of these textbooks was Vicki Ruiz and Ellen DuBois's *Unequal Sisters*, first issued in 1990 and now in its fourth edition. Interestingly, this compilation was marketed as a source book in women's history that paid attention to gender and other axes of identity, especially race and ethnicity.

The textbook featured selections on class and gender violence, race, Mexican immigrant women, Chinese American women, Black women in the Midwest, and more. Equally interesting is the way that the term "intersectional" was inflected as "multicultural" in the original subtitle and, by the fourth edition, had morphed into "inclusive." That said, a reviewer of the first edition urged caution, noting that of the two dozen or so chapters, three focused on Indigenous women, four on Asian American women, and five each on African American women and Latinas. "The rest are on specific topics reflecting the experiences of largely white women across class, cultural, political, or theoretical lines." Regardless, women's history "has no choice from this point forward except to offer... multicultural perspectives." For their part, Ruiz and Dubois argued early on for the use of "multicultural" over "multiracial" because it displaced white history from center stage.

In the US context at least, how much of the stage gender should occupy in relation to race and ethnicity was a live question. This was due in part to the institutionalization and growth of ethnic studies programs in US colleges and universities and, often, the proximity of those units to programs in women's and gender studies. Though all local histories tell their own stories, all of these programs emerged sooner or later from civil rights and related struggles in communities of color across the United States. In that sense, where and when intersectionality in the scholarly work came to bear on gender history, it had ties to, if not roots in, 1960s and 1970s activism and its legacies well into the late twentieth century.

The political work and writing of a figure like Angela Davis— whose involvement in radical Black politics, including arrest, trial, and imprisonment, made her an international phenomenon in that same period—was critical to the globalization of intersectional thinking and scholarship, not least through her 1981 book, *Women, Race and Class*. That collection of essays brought critical attention to Black feminism and its critique of white patriarchy through a rewriting of American history which made clear that to see all three categories together was an act of revolution. In fact, later reviews deemed it intersectional analysis, though it was written before the term was in wide circulation in US scholarship. As late as 2000, which saw the publication of Siobhan Somerville's field-changing *Queering the Color Line*, the institutional organization of research and teaching on race and gender, and race and sexuality, was, if not segregated, then arguably siloed and undertaken separately.

What approaches came to the fore as the field took off beyond its founding moment? Two books by scholars from the post-1995 PhD generation of gender historians underscore both the continued urgency of compound thinking when it came to gender history and the ways in which the field was pushed in new directions by scholars who wanted to think intentionally about sexuality, normative and otherwise. Judy Wu's 2005 study of Margaret Chung, widely regarded as the first American-born Chinese female physician, looked to biography as a way of showing how one life, seen through an intersectional prism, could illuminate some of the hidden transcripts of US history. This twin purpose was the explicit motivation of the book: "How did Chung accomplish what she did in her professional, political, and personal life? And how do her experiences provide insight into the historical transformation of American norms regarding race, gender, and sexuality over the course of her lifetime?"

Race and gender norms, the relationship between race and ethnicity and sexuality, between gender and sexuality and nationality, between gender and cultural persona, between race

Miss Margaret Chung

5. This image of Margaret "Mom" Chung appeared in the *Los Angeles Register* in 1914 and reflects her celebrity as the first known Chinese American woman medical doctor. She was known to adopt what was then considered "masculine" dress. She later worked as a recruiter of pilots in the Second World War.

and gender-appropriate behavior—all of these analytics, with their shifting lenses and their historical situatedness in a modernizing, imperializing, and segregationist United States, shape Wu's account of "Dr. Mom," whose life spans the late nineteenth century through the postwar period. Chung wore what was then considered masculine attire in medical school and had romantic relationships with several women, facts that were largely unknown during her lifetime, either despite or because of what was practically national celebrity for her war efforts. Knowledge of Chung's intimate life or experience—the deep recesses where gender, race, sexuality, and the specificity of time and place promise more then we can make them deliver—eludes Wu, though she respectfully imagines where she can.

Nayan Shah takes up similar questions in his 2012 *Stranger Intimacy*, braiding gender status and roles with questions of immigration and erotics, racial subordination and subcultures, atypical comportment and national identity, the law and state legitimacy—here in the cross-border context of the United States and Canada, and of "Asiatic," "Oriental," and otherwise othered male migrants. This is queer intersectional history grounded in the complex politics of gender on the move, where binaries have symbolic and material force but are jostled and remade through the collision of some bodies with particular regimes of labor, domesticity, consent, and, of course, a culture of sexual violence. Early twentieth-century newspapers baldly "combined economic competition with gender defamation" in their analyses of what they deemed racial crisis: "Every day, whites are being replaced in the mills by Asiatics. The invaders have become bold and insolent, [with] many instances of women being pushed into the gutters, insulted on street cars."

We hear echoes here of Deborah Gray White's southern "ladydom" endangered by racialized subordinates, and evidence of men highly "modified" (recall Morgan) by race while (white) women are not. Above all, we see how gender both structures alternative sodalities and, under the conditions of white colonial frontier settlement, is utterly undone and recomposed by them. Shah shows, effectively, how the ties that bound South Asian migrants both challenged *and* upheld the social norms that emerged in the fraught racial landscape of US borderlands. Gender was not necessarily primary among those norms, yet it was undoubtedly historically consequential nonetheless. Gender is, in specific times and places, the modality in which race is lived.

As race and gender moved together to the fore in histories committed to intersectional research methods and narrative strategies, then, we find scholars more carefully calibrating the work—we might even say the sovereignty—of gender as a carrier of discourse and a material driver of what happens, and how, in the past. Indeed, with even a quick glance at the categories big and small through which historians have written and taught since the 1990s (from the nation to the prison, from domesticity to diplomacy), we can see that gender as a carrier, and/or an effect, of *multiple* striations of power has had to be reckoned with. But this is not a triumphalist narrative. We might look to the surge in new histories of disability in the mid-2000s to begin to appreciate how unevenly intersectionality played out. Scholars of disability took quickly to gender as a category of analysis, but have been slower to think, and to design their research, with multiple axes of identity at the center.

The move toward truly interconnected histories as a best practice speaks to the shifting grounds upon which gender history sought a foothold as the politics, and the geopolitics, of the twenty-first century influenced the terms and conditions under which professional history of all kinds was conceived and written. If gender history had been no exception, this is perhaps a sign of its arrival, if not its absorption into the slipstream. Nowhere is this more legible than in the scholarship on empire, colonialism, and transnationalism that has gained ground in the Western academy since the beginning of the breakup of the postwar, Cold War world order (which we can date, alongside the emergence of neoliberalism, in and around the 1970s).

Four key titles will suffice to make the point. The first, Philippa Levine's 2003 *Prostitution, Race, and Politics: Policing Venereal Disease in the British Empire*, put a stake in the ground that was long in coming. She argued, through a series of case studies emerging from archival research that was as irrefutable as it was impressive, that imperial politics was sexual politics by any other name, and that the official record itself revealed the entanglement of gender and race politics from the palace of Whitehall to the lowliest (and loneliest) colonial outpost. Her keywords were "gender and civilization," "colonialism," "gender and race," "gender, race and policy," "gender and racial health," "gender, the body and disease," "gender and racial difference," and "gender and the racializing of space." The geographical reach of the study (India, Hong Kong, the Straits Settlements) challenged a mere metropole/colony approach and underscored how a focus on prostitution as both racialized and gendered sex work politely exploded any claims to an Island Story in the age of empire. And though it is often discussed in service of a broader points comparison across colonial sites, Levine's contention that whiteness itself was an effect of the collision of gendered and racialized bodies in the imperial marketplace of sex was an example for many readers of the intersectionality of gender history hiding in plain sight.

Scholars working closely with colonial archives found that they yielded new histories of masculinity that could not be understood except through the conjuncture of gender with race and sexual identity. That is, colonial modernity itself had to be historicized in and through evidence of the degenerate and feminized East as a foil to its virile, white European counterpart. Departing from what he felt was Edward Said's insufficiently historicized notions of orientalism (which certainly wore gender lightly), Wilson Chacko Jacob's 2011 *Working Out Egypt* argues for masculinity as a site for the creation of the modern nationalist subject in the nineteenth and twentieth centuries. His focus is urban Cairo, and his study is motivated in the broadest sense by the question of how Egypt's encounter with colonialism occasioned the emergence of new forms of social and cultural discipline around the male body. In the process, Jacob reimagines occupied Egypt not just as a site where hegemonic imperial masculinity of the kind articulated by Lords Cromer and Kitchener was transplanted, but as a terrain on which new forms of nationalist expression pivoted on an anticolonial model of how to be a modern Egyptian middle-class/ professional man—in behavior, dress, public address, and political imagination. The result is a vigorously argued, carefully researched account of how regimes of gender, class, and Anglo-Saxon racialism converged to shape the very basis of modern nationalism in the shadow of empire. In a notable turn of phrase (borrowed from the term for a clerical corps in the Ottoman bureaucracy), Jacob calls this performance of cultural cosmopolitanism "effendi masculinity."

The challenge of assessing the experiences of the colonized in imperial and transnational histories is akin to that of calibrating the appropriate weight of gender—whether lived through ethnicity, age, status, linguistic community—for many scholars of empire and the history of the global. Two studies that take an intersectional approach to interracial relationships in very different parts of the world underscore the limits of gender history, like all history, when it comes to much of what we really want to know of the past. Angela Wanhalla's *Matters of the Heart* (2013) focuses on marriage in white settler New Zealand, where the practice was expressly bound up in state policies of racial amalgamation—a policy that had the eradication of Māori marriage conventions and tradition squarely in mind. Alive to the resonance of the connection between interracial marriage and "good race relations" in Brazil and elsewhere, Wanhalla nonetheless reads closely for how legal expectations and cultural practice operated in tense and tender relationship to one another in colonial New Zealand. She does this by discerning patterns of cohabitation and concubinage in order to make clear how colonial projects drew on pathologized notions of Indigenous gender practice even as they generated new forms of expectations for Māori women in the process.

Tracking the spaces and places where gender is the idiom in which race is lived leads Wanhalla to scenes like the one said to have taken place as the ship *Dromedary* arrived in the Bay of Islands in 1820. The son of the vessel's master allegedly tried to seduce the sister-in-law of a local chief, offering her a nail as a token of his intentions, even though she told him she was not free, as she was the wife of another man. When it was discovered that she had kept the nail, the onus was on her to prove she had done nothing criminal. Here, as in so many other places where the desire for intersectional approaches outstrips the reality of the colonial archive, evidence of Māori women's own experiences and emotional lives is scant. The very trace itself is suggestive of the limits of our historical knowledge—of what Jennifer Morgan calls the outright unknowability of the past.

And yet in the context of empire history where gender is a subject—and despite the limits of the archive—historians have worked mightily to make the impact of exploitative sexual regimes on colonized men and women visible wherever possible. Carina Ray's *Crossing the Color Line: Race, Sex, and the Contested Politics of Colonialism in Ghana* (2015) is rooted in West Africa even as it ranges adventurously across the continent, using a wide-angle Anglophone empire lens to think broadly and adeptly about the similarities and differences between colonies, and to historicize the fate of sexual liaisons against the grain of transnational imperial change in the twentieth century as well. Ray's study is remarkable for the scrupulous attention she pays to the embeddedness of sexual relations in local contexts. She excavates textured personal stories and offers fine-grained analyses of how race and gender and class intertwined to produce African agency alongside growing British unease. And the evidence of panic, uncertainty, and what Ray calls imperial "maladministration" in the face of everyday challenges to the racialized sexual order the British sought to impose reminds us that gender has agency in history, if we learn how to see it.

Ray manages the question of change over time exceedingly well, making this a truly and deeply historical account of interracial sex in Africa, where, as she notes, scholarship on the subject has tended more toward the sociology of race and gender than that of history per se. Moreover, she makes a persuasive case for the indispensability of such history to any account of imperial power and ambition, suggesting what a drag gender and sexual intimacy across the color line could be on colonial and newly postcolonial control. Like all of the scholars who grapple with intersectionality, and with the question of what degree of primacy to afford gender in history, Ray aims for the biggest historical canvas possible, often through a kaleidoscope of gendered lives lived in conditions of racial inequality and subjugation. On now to what happens when the turn of that kaleidoscope propels us beyond the West and before the modern, and to what that means for the viability of gender history in those arenas.

# Chapter 4
# Before the modern, beyond the Americas

Gender history emerged as a professional practice and a subfield of the discipline in the Western academy during an extended moment of later-twentieth-century global conflict and change. Some of those conflicts left their imprint on scholarly debates about the work of gender—debates that derived in part from what sounded, to some, like universalist assumptions built into how gender was conceived of and mobilized. The work of intersectional theory and practice questioned the singularity of gender's power as a category of historical analysis. This was and is, in turn, a powerful challenge to "gender history" itself, which appears to accord a central role to gender.

Yet in practice, and ever since its origins, scholars in the field have striven to countenance a variety of forms of difference and to work through what those differences have meant for people's lived experiences. While many historians of gender came to operate intersectionally, bringing race, class, and sexuality to bear on their research and their narratives, the politics of what the primacy of gender signaled for the practice of gender history was a point of contention in debates about both the subfield and the wider practices in the profession of history. In light of the far-ranging nature of these debates, we can see gender history's impact beyond its immediate ken and appreciate the role it has played in animating important conversations about the premises of historical thinking writ large.

Much of the critique of gender history's tendency to subsume racial difference came from scholars working at the intersection of social movements and intellectual traditions steeped in histories of racism, racial violence, and colonialism, with particular emphasis on African American and Black politics worldwide. These critics, often scholars of women, slavery, and post-emancipation histories, sought to draw attention to established assumptions about how femininity and masculinity worked: norms shaped by presumptively white middle-class standards in which gender was entailed. For some, the universalist meanings that gender history was in danger not just of carrying but of reproducing as "normal" revealed the racial politics of gender history as an ongoing, ontological problem, tied to its origins in the Anglo-American academy and especially to the influence of its American practitioners.

In the introduction to their 2007 roundtable on gendering transnational historiographies, Karen Hagemann (a German historian) and Maria Teresa Fernández-Aceves (a Mexican historian) noted that "non-American women's and gender historians, particularly those from non-English-speaking nations, often find themselves in a paradoxical situation. Drawn to a feminist scholarship that exposes power structures and emphasizes diversity in experience and perspective, they are ultimately confronted with academic hierarchies that require them to write in English and to adhere to an established Anglo-American style of presenting research if they hope to gain an audience in the dominant English-speaking academic community of feminist scholars. Gender and women's history thus stands," they concluded, "in consistent danger of losing its international and intellectual diversity."

Significant is their call to recognize "power structures" and "hierarchies" within the field. Interesting, too, is the way they paired women's and gender history as equally shaped by these fields of power, as equally implicated in the politics of representation and of uneven development that resonated with global political trends with deep histories.

The historical coincidence of the rise of gender history with the institutionalization of global studies across the disciplines in the last decades of the twentieth century meant that historians of gender had to grapple with increasingly multisited approaches to their subject, and to think about intersectionality in a number of different ways, especially when it came to space and place. For although it was not until the mid-2010s that gender history was thought to "go global," we know that scholars had long been doing interconnected work, seeing patterns and making links across time and space with the question of how masculinity and femininity worked in those dimensions always in view. And yet the global is not a view from nowhere. As the feminist lesbian poet Adrienne Rich reminded us, we have to ask the question, "Where do we see it from?" In this context, we may take this question as grounds for asking historians of gender to remember our own subject positions—our own situatedness in time and space—as we design our research tools and methodologies. And to remain vigilant about the power of the global to erase women and gender in the name of working "at scale."

Marilyn Booth, a scholar of histories of women and gender in the Arabic world, exhorts us to bring this critical vantage point perspective to the geopolitics of gender when she asks, "How might 'the self' look different not only across distinctions of gender identity and over time but also when we read from other places—and depending on where we stand as we listen?" That same situational approach enables us to explore the consequences for gender history when we read gender through the lens of modern Western norms and assumptions. Gender historians themselves have called attention to what happens when we naturalize modern Western identities and conditions as the grounds upon which we devise our assumptions about what gender is and how it works, rather than considering how gender history is actually produced through those assumptions.

Scholars of times and places "before the modern" have long understood the ways in which concepts of the modern and modernity itself are the very grammar of history. That is, there is a "chronological chauvinism" to Western history as a practice, one that assumes a progression from barbarism to enlightenment— even when postmodern and postcolonial critiques would appear to have laid such fantastical imaginings to rest. The persistence of periodization techniques and terms such as "ancient," "medieval," "early modern," and "postmodern" contribute to this perception that historical change is linear and bending toward the arc of improvement—and that the conditions of that betterment are universally understood to resemble (if not derive from) from modern European norms and standards. The implicit and explicit conviction about the superiority of the modern is hard to discount, in part because it is effectively ubiquitous. Suffice it to say that even historians who recognize the modern as a contested, if not also flawed, historiographical concept concede that one definition of it is a capacity for "cultural reflexivity" and complex thinking.

Even if we acknowledge that turning such reflexivity on the modern itself is also a sign of modernity, it is hard not to grant that a belief in hierarchies of thinking means modernity for some and backwardness for others. And such backwardness has a temporal charge, a connotation of lag or drag, a flatness and a state of underdevelopment all too easily designated as "primitive." Even the descriptor "before the modern" participates in the logic historians of these times work hard to exceed. As one historian of medieval Mexico has put it, "invoking the modern is never a natural or inconsequential affair, but a violent regulatory speech act." Clearly there are links between the way historians mobilize the modern and the way they have configured the non-West. Indeed, as medievalists have been at special pains to show, history is a project of "occupying other peoples' territories and times," and not just metaphorically.

The synergies between ancient civilization and patriarchy are conventional wisdom now, but gender historians were keen from the start to emphasize the importance of identifying patterns of difference and similarity across various kinds of polities in the "preclassical" period. They were also invested in investigating what might look like self-evident relations between women and a gendered institution like marriage, and to underscore the necessity of not looking through modernist lenses. The continuum of goddesses, whores, wives, and slaves proposed early on by Sarah Pomeroy suggests a concerted effort to resist easy binaries and to think of how gender relations shaped who counted as a woman. Or, for that matter, what counted as manly. What's more, evidence from the ancient world does not always confirm to the either/or thinking that structures the modern sex/gender binary—and often challenges it. And significantly, premodern patriarchal systems did not always tell the whole story of gender relations. Confucianism, which was long credited with creating a gender system that cast women as weak and irrational and men as wise and reasonable, did not necessarily map directly onto lived realities.

One way of assessing the gap between binary logics and social life on the ground is to say that, in some times and places, gender dominance has been aspirational, and that systems that developed before the machinery of the nation-state were potentially more porous and open to transgression, evasion, or indifference. Where the evidence is available, that interpretation might well hold for local societies and world-scale systems in advance of European hegemony. Yet what Merry Wiesner-Hanks calls "gendered temporalities" is something different. She suggests that while gender may be a dimension of historical experience, it is also produced by the specific pressures of the historical moment through which it is emerging—in ways that help decide what forms it does or does not take. Of course, there are many approaches to historicizing this phenomenon, as Wiesner-Hanks's own career-long body of work testifies. The gendered histories of material objects, of female communities, of family configurations, of wondrous "hairy girls"—these are all entrées into accounts of how and why "gender," whether as a fixed binary or a fluid terrain, is never simply found in history but is produced in and by it.

The classroom has, unsurprisingly, been a rich and productive space for bringing these issues to the fore. A syllabus that has gotten a lot of attention for some of these questions is the one that Heidi Tinsman and Ulrike Strasser published in the pedagogy section of the journal *Radical History Review* in 2005, based on their experience of coteaching a world history course in the University of California system called "World History, Gender and Politics, 1400–1870." Strasser is an early modern Europeanist, Tinsman a historian of modern Latin America. They came together to teach a course and developed a syllabus that, they recounted, emerged "out of our commitment as feminists to making gender and sexuality central to how the rapidly growing field of world history is being shaped." Among the topics included were the centrality of sexuality and religion to conquest and rule in Mesoamerica and Europe; the role of female seclusion and state formation in Europe, China, and the Middle East; the significance of slavery and its gendered divisions of labor to local economies and the emergence of capitalism; the gender-specific meanings of citizenship and nation; and the part played by imperialism in sexualizing and racializing women's and men's bodies.

The course also recognized the tyranny of the modern as a problem for and of gender history. The instructors toggled between the Americas and Europe, and between the Americas and Asia—part of their investment in challenging Europe as the protagonist of world history regardless of temporality. And they emphasized the radical history of Incan gender by citing and teaching the work of Irene Silverblatt, whose *Moon, Sun, and Witches* (1987) shows "how the Inca transformed Andean cosmology's emphasis on parallel and roughly equivalent gender roles into a cosmology of gender hierarchy that emphasized female subordination as a metaphor for Andean submission to Inca rule." In other words, gender difference and gender hierarchies were not a given in this early modern context, as they were not across time before the modern, when capitalism and other forces hardened masculinity and femininity into warring factions in the realms of identity and representation, but also in spaces of labor and commerce and religious practice. It is impossible to know how students received this plotline. But it suggests how scholarship and teaching on periods before, say, the nineteenth and twentieth centuries offer opportunities to denaturalize modern assumptions about gender difference—to rethink and reimagine how time conditions the way gender operates, and how it does not.

Carol Symes's insightful take on the inseparability of the time of the modern and the time of the West is helpful for appreciating what is at stake for gender history beyond Europe and the United States. In her view, the people of the so-called Middle Ages "inhabit a conceptual space analogous to that of 'India' in the British colonial imagination." For just as "the British conquered and represented the diversity of 'Indian' pasts through a homogenizing narrative of transition from a 'medieval' period to 'modernity,' so Modern Europeans and their imitators squeezed the diversity of 'medieval' pasts into a homogenizing narrative of barbarity from which they, qua modern people, had liberated themselves. To take on the role of medievalist is consequently— and all unwillingly—to become a minor colonial official whose job depends on maintaining the subaltern status of the population under scrutiny."

In support of her point, and citing Gayatri Spivak's well-known postcolonial feminist provocation, "Can the Subaltern Speak?," Symes contends that "the word 'medieval' can be substituted for 'subaltern' in nearly every sentence of Spivak's essay with no distortion of sense. There is a similar range of possible answers to 'Can the medieval speak?'"

Analogs to this question abound in the field. Is the hegemony of the modern in historical practice akin to that of gender in the doing of gender history? Was the concept of gender imported by the West? As the sociologist Oyèrónkẹ́ Oyěwùmí has trenchantly observed, "I came to realize that the fundamental category 'woman'—which is foundational in Western gender discourse— simply did not exist in Yorubaland, prior to sustained contact with the West. There is no such preexisting group characterized by shared interests, desires, or social position." Can gender history be understood as a vehicle for the colonizing work of modern Western accounts of the past? Is there an "empire of gender" to which Indigenous cosmologies are routinely subjected?

The work of Afsaneh Najmabadi is exemplary on this point. In *Women with Mustaches and Men without Beards* (2005), she recounts coming to grips with the serious limitations of operating with gender, and the gender binary, as a Western-based category in the context of Iranian anxieties about modernity. She encountered both vocabulary and visual imagery in the archives that refused the gender analysis with which she arrived. That refusal is not simply a resistance to interpretation, nor is it a bad fit. It is rather a recognition that the way Western history had assumed gender to work could not be accommodated in the context of modern Iran. By her own account, Najmabadi was no naïf when she began her project. She went into the research fully determined to make the point that gender history could be done, and that it had profound significance for histories that had never taken it into account.

But she was caught up unexpectedly short. As she frankly tells it, the book began as a project on gender in the formation of Iranian modernity on iconic, narrative, metaphoric, and social levels. "But I had overlooked another labor of gender: its production as a binary, man/woman. Thinking of gender as man/woman turned out to be a very modern imperative. I had overlooked the erasures that made this binarity of gender possible in the first place." As she reread and rethought the entire project, she realized that she had to confront the fact that the man/woman binary did not operate in the same way in the Iranian context as in the Western one, nor could the gendered frame of analysis she had in mind be transported wholesale.

What Najmabadi came to understand is that the "gender" in gender history functions as a carrier of unexamined and unwritten histories of encounter, imperialism, and settlement in ways that can be obscured unless we acknowledge that the field has taken many Western assumptions—about the binary of man/woman, among other things—for granted as universal, rather than as the product of Western imperial histories. As she goes on to relate, what made her project, and indeed potentially any project, of gender history inherently challenging is that "gender as a binary has since become a template for categories of modern sexuality. Our contemporary binary of gender translates any fractures of masculinity into effeminization. Nineteenth-century Iranian culture, however, had other terms, such as *amrad* (young adolescent male) and *mukhannas* (an adult man desiring to be an object of desire for adult men), that were not equated with effeminacy." In other words, Najmabadi's experience of trying to write gender history in a non-Western context reminds us that the male/female binary can operate as a colonial idiom, that what the Argentine feminist philosopher Maria Lugones calls the "coloniality of gender" is one inheritance of modern global geopolitics—and of history writing.

Is gender history—because it is directly and indirectly a product of colonial modernity—prone to replicating these erasures and the violence that they entail? Historians who research and write about formerly colonized places have certainly been mindful of the possibility. As early as 1989, Nancy Rose Hunt observed that "at its most insidious, the literature on collective action is marked by a tendency to use African women's political protest and rebellion as a means of articulating western feminist strategies. The search for 'feminist consciousness' among African women has led to the imposition of categories such as patriarchy and solidarity on their experienced assessments of whether class or gender is the primary motivating factor of women's political activities and distortion or neglect of African women's own perceptions, motives, divisions and memories." At the same time, Hunt wondered why histories of women and gender in Africa were not following more closely on the lines of US and European work. She argued that there is a need to "'en-gender' African history, to look not only at differences between men and women, but at differences among and within women and at how, in Joan Scott's words, 'history has been enacted on the field of gender.'"

Almost two decades later, the emphasis was on gender history on the ground in Africa. The editors of the provocatively titled 2007 collection *Africa After Gender?* treat gender as a historical agent that acts in African contexts through local contexts—as masculinity and as femininity—but cast an intentional eye on "knowledge about gender in Africa that is also *produced* in Africa," citing this as "an essential point of view, a necessary corrective" (emphasis in original). Meanwhile, Mutiat Oladejo observed that in the case of Nigeria, prominent female historians such as Bolanle Awe, Nina Mba, and LaRay Denzer struggled mightily against institutional resistance. Thanks to their efforts, the Women's Research and Documentation Centre (WORDOC) was established in Ibadan in 1987, though more as an interdisciplinary effort than as a strictly historical one. As late as 2018 Oladejo concluded that "with greater access to resources, U.S. and

European scholars publish more about Africans than do African scholars." Meanwhile, first- and second-generation scholars of African descent take up African women's and gender history in the US academy, but it is comparatively rare for Western scholarly journals to publish work originating from gender historians on the continent.

As Jean Allman remarked in the wake of her 2018 presidential address to the African Studies Association, Africanist scholars trained after World War II have more typically than not operated inside structures of US academic power and privilege. Historians of gender beyond the West have been no exception. For better or worse, the often rancorous debates in their respective fields about who is making and doing history have made the fault lines between North and South more visible. Though this is a history yet to be written, it is interesting to consider what role the production of histories of gendered hierarchies of race, class, and sexuality have contributed to the nature and tenor of those debates. Meanwhile, those who work on geographies outside of the United States and Europe often have a more vigorous skepticism about the wholesale applicability of the gender in "gender and history"—or perhaps they are simply more vocal about it.

Tani Barlow's work on the question of women in Chinese feminism is uncannily in sync with Najmabadi on gender and Iranian modernity, in that she is as interested in the category of women as she is in the ways that that category itself was historically produced. Rooted in fine-grained linguistic analysis, her goal is to underscore how untranslatable English words like "women" and "gender" are in non-Western lexicons. Elizabeth LaCouture does similarly careful work around the highly gendered concept of domesticity, which is not a Chinese concept—it did not translate self-evidently, it was routed through Japanese and later American sources, and it never really took root as the anchor of gender ideology. LaCouture puts it succinctly and pointedly when she remarks that "[t]he history of translating 'domesticity' into Chinese thus reveals that Euro-American historiographical terms that were once thought to be universal map poorly onto other places and suggests that we need more inclusive frames for comparative gender history." Of note is the fact that Barlow had been sounding the alarm about the predominance of Western paradigms since the 1980s, and in the pages of *Gender and History* as well.

Not all histories that touch on gender beyond Europe and the Americas contour ineluctably to gender history's Western modernist impulses. Gender history in and of India (as elsewhere, commonly paired with women's history in related review essays and collections) has long worked in dialogic relationship with the history of empire on the subcontinent. Among many possible representatives of this work, Mrinalini Sinha's *Specters of Mother India* (2006) stands out for its deft negotiation of the relationships between gender as a category of social identity and "the social domain of Indian gender relations" in the context of feminism, nationalism, and imperialism. In a subtle nod to a Scottian take on the capacity of gender history to demonstrate the historical processes whereby gender is produced, she argues that "the collective mobilization of women qua women authorized new gendered subjectivities for women" in modes that were to prove consequential for the direction of both colonial and postcolonial politics. Sinha's attention to caste and class, as well as to the impossibility of disentangling interwar Indian political modernity from its imperial contexts, means that, in her capable hands, gender history shows us the consequences of that entanglement as perhaps no other optic could.

By the same token, not all Indian gender history engages so directly with the colonial state or imperial political culture. Tanika Sarkar's 1999 study, *Words to Win*, offers a deeply researched and reflective history of the making of *Amar Jiban*, the first modern Bengali autobiography, which happens to be written by a woman.

6. Though the dominant image of the suffragette is of the white English woman chaining herself to the radiators in the Houses of Parliament, Indian women also transgressed gender boundaries and made claims in public for their right to the vote in both India and Britain. This group marched as part of the Women's Coronation Procession in London in 1911.

It shows how gender history tacks back and forth through this woman's history, with the Raj barely in sight. Elsewhere, and specifically in the context of child marriage and age of consent, Sarkar strikes a prudent and instructive balance when it comes to the proportional role of imperial power in modern India. Her *Hindu Wife, Hindu Nation* (which does not, interestingly, mention gender in the title) shows how a gender history of law "sustains a reexamination of the relationship between individual legal rights, community norms and citizenship rights as they were configured under colonial rule." It is thus eminently possible to do gender history without reinscribing modern Western gender norms either narratively or methodologically—while accounting for imperial modernity all the same.

It is, admittedly, difficult to see, and to keep at front of mind, how and why the practice of gender history is always part of a "world picture." That's because stories of how gender works are still highly naturalized. Which is to say, his/stories of gender reproduce scripts of gender history that carry unexamined assumptions we fail to recognize or unpick. Emily Martin's 1991 essay "The Egg and the Sperm" is a very effective way of helping students interested in the basics of gender history grasp this rather meta, but critical, point. She rehearses three revisionist accounts of the story how of the egg and the sperm make their way to fertilization in textbooks designed for medical students at Johns Hopkins University. Despite successive waves of new research underscoring the agency of the sperm and imagining a new dynamism in the egg, a heterosexual romance narrative of a particular kind continues to obtain. Even revisionist accounts of egg and sperm could not get beyond established hierarchies.

For despite the fact that each new account gave the egg a larger and more active role, taken together they bring into play another cultural stereotype: woman as a dangerous and aggressive threat. New data did not, in other words, lead scientists "to eliminate gender stereotypes in their descriptions of egg and sperm. Instead, scientists simply began to describe egg and sperm in different, but no less damaging, terms. [New research] clearly . . . shows that the egg and sperm do interact on more mutual terms, making biology's refusal to portray them that way all the more disturbing."

Martin ends by admitting that there is no easy solution, because the biggest challenge in this particular narrative context is not to assign the egg and the sperm personhood. Failing that, she argues, we need to "wake up our metaphors" and be "aware of when we are projecting cultural imagery onto what we study, . . . by becoming aware of their implications, we will rob them of their power to naturalize our social conventions about gender."

Historians of gender working before modernity or beyond the West already know that the conditions of those times and places mean they need to be alive to ready-made metaphors and even reckon with some of their own. It may be a bridge too far to say that the gender in gender history colonizes, though some version of that story is implicit in the ways that scholars who do not work squarely in the European and American contexts have talked about the work in even an unruly subfield like this one. Wherever scholars naturalize modern Western contexts and conditions rather than interrogating how gender is actually produced through them, and through their assumptions about what defines men and women, there is the chance that gender history is part of the problem rather than a true challenge to the protocols of the craft.

To stay with this challenge takes some self-consciousness about the ways in which gender history is itself an agent in the production of knowledge—a force that not only resides in social relations but is shaped itself by the array of historical forces that have accompanied its emergence as a field. It has been something of an agent in histories of Western dominance, imperialism, hegemony, and crisis as well. At stake in this recognition is the potential of gender history to disrupt rather than simply mirror dominant systems of power whose pasts and presents it aims to throw into question.

# Chapter 5
# Queering the subject

Though it is tempting to represent the story of gender history as a series of revisionary moments on the way to a more progressive present, that has not been the trajectory of the field, which has actually been a terrain upon which debates over the limits and possibilities of gender itself have been continually worked out—with profound implications for the discipline of history itself. Along the way, gender history has been continuously, productively unsettled by the variety of historical forces that have shaped the time and place of its emergence in the academy. It has channeled the social and political conflicts of its moment, offering us a unique vantage point from which to observe how the inheritances of the past have weighed on it, and why the histories of the present continue to influence the directions it takes.

Nowhere is this more evident, perhaps, than in the provocations to gender history posed by queer critiques. As with the challenges from intersectional thinkers, from non-Western scholars, and from historians working before the modern period, queer takes on gender did not follow serially from a foundational or well-established field of gender history. For though queer interventions have been galvanized by political activism and shaped by local and global histories in recent collective memory, they are hardly latecomers to gender history. Like claims about the fundamental role of race, they were there from the start. Because the narrative of liberal progress is so rooted in ideas of emancipation from gender stereotypes, the fact that queer challenges to gender history are not the historical successors to the field cannot be overemphasized. For while they have built on early work in the field, often in vocal opposition to, say, the presumption of a gender binary, scholars invested in queering gender were part of gender history from its origins as an academic subject—often before they were labeled as such.

What's more, queer history, theory, and studies have been marked by many of the same social and political crises as gender history per se: as fields of inquiry, they, too, have been variously US-centric, presumptively white, and skewing modern. The fact that these fields share such basic properties speaks to fact that they emerged with gender history rather than after it. In that sense, queer history cannot be said to have followed from it, or moved beyond it, regardless of the political desires we may have for that kind of progressive story.

Judith Butler's influential study *Gender Trouble* was published in 1990—that is, effectively, at the same moment that *Gender and History* launched the academic field and Kimberlé Crenshaw first published on the concept of intersectionality. Butler's retrospective account of her intentions in *Gender Trouble* is instructive: "I sought to counter those views that made presumptions about the limits and propriety of gender and restricted the meaning of gender to received notions of masculinity and femininity." The aim of *Gender Trouble* was "to open up the field of possibility for gender without dictating which kinds of possibilities ought to be realized."

Central to Butler's arguments is the contention that gender is produced by the political and cultural conditions in which it finds itself rather than being antecedent to them, and that it operates performatively, even improvisationally, in ways dependent on those particular conditions. "To understand gender as a historical category," she argues, "is to accept that gender, understood as one way of culturally configuring a body, is open to a continual remaking," and that "anatomy" and "sex" are not immune to the impact of the cultural frames that condition them.

Although she did not address the field of gender history per se in *Gender Trouble*, the contingency of time and place is arguably critical to Butler's theory of gender trouble, as is intersectionality (what she called "the racial, class, ethnic, sexual and regional modalities of discursively constituted identities"). And while she did not specifically invoke gender as a category of analysis in the first edition, categorical thinking—about women, gender, sexuality, and identity—pervades the text. This resort to categories had its own feminist history; in the words of Monique Wittig, for example, "the category of sex is the political category that founds society as heterosexual." Meanwhile, Joan Scott's 1986 essay, which was still relatively recent and just gathering the momentum that would propel it into the center of the field, is cited in chapter 1 of *Gender Trouble*. And in an echo of Scott's argument in the tenth edition, Butler asks, "How do non-normative sexual practices call into question the stability of *gender as a category of analysis*? How do certain sexual practices compel the question: what is a woman, what is a man?"(italics in the original).

The social history of the intellectual life of these times has yet to be written, but some of the conversations and intellectual alliances can be traced through debates at the intersection of gender theory and gender history. Though I have not conducted a citation count, I don't believe that Butler's work had as much of an impact on historians as Scott. But she did help to stage encounters between queer theory and the history of gender that have gone a long way toward querying the tendency to binary thinking in the field. Nancy Cott named the problem when she said that "gender history not only recognizes women as historical agents but also revokes the assumption that men are neuter beings whose masculinity and sexuality require no notice. This perspective presumes that every

historical subject is shaped and influenced by gender attributes—
and by the existence of a gender binary."

The practice of historicizing that binary is a major preoccupation
of the field, of course. But scholars have always been equally
invested in understanding the limits of the binary: the contexts
where it was in flux, where that fluidity was regulated and
punished, the silences and erasures that ensued—and the ways in
which traditional politics, culture, economics, religion, and more
made and remade themselves by closing out and shutting down
the historical possibilities of gender "trouble." In that sense,
gender history's preoccupations were and are broadly consonant
with Butler's insistence that "to understand gender as a historical
category... is to accept that gender, understood as one way of
culturally configuring a body, is open to a continual remaking."

At the same time, and notably, the subtitle of *Gender Trouble* is
*Feminism and the Subversion of Identity*. Gender historians have
undoubtedly been interested in gender identity, though the
emphasis in the field, especially in its first decades, was on those
historical processes that created gender difference rather than
those by which gender binaries were subverted or undone. One
way of thinking about this is to say that gender history has most
often been a space to test out how and why gender binaries
operated, with what consequences, and for whom. Where gender's
instability was at issue was at the site of differences—race, class,
ethnicity, ability—that challenged the explanatory power of gender
as *the* category of historical analysis.

Queering the subject suggests something related but different. It
means recognizing the work of gender binaries in guaranteeing
compulsory heterosexuality; in other words, we must admit that
normative sexuality fortifies normative gender, and vice versa.
Queering the subject of gender also means acknowledging that
gender identity is a fiction, albeit a powerful one, because it is
never fixed, but is rather involved in processes of continual

remaking—not just *across* different times and places, but also in the spaces *between* the gender that is assigned and the gender that is performed. Pursuit of that drag effect, rather than of the gender binary itself, might be said to distinguish gender history from its queer counterparts.

It would be a mistake to reduce any practice to one or the other, or to suggest that there is a reigning standard for inclusion or exclusion in any category we might name to describe the work of making histories of gender(s) available to academics and wider publics. But in the spirit of introductory definitions, one might say that not all gender history is necessarily queer history—that is, it is not all invested in subjects who might be identified as queer or operating from queer methodologies of researching and reading. But queer history is arguably a form of gender history by any other name. That peculiar kinship has meant that these approaches have coexisted and have informed each other for several decades.

The first history labeled queer to be published in *Gender and History* was in 1997: Dan Healey used case studies from the Stalinist period to track how "revolutionary socialist respectability" mapped onto conventional expectations about marriage and family. Articles and book reviews quickly abounded, led by Matt Houlbrook's study on "Lady Austin's Camp Boys," which told the sensational story of police raids on a London ballroom frequented by cross-dressers, in service of a larger argument about how those caught up in it were framed as "queer subjects." Houlbrook argued that the ensuing trial "inscribed the defendants within pejorative categories of gender abnormality, defining a real man through what he ought not to be." Moreover, he suggested that the authorities read "male gender inversion as *both* a threat to established gender norms *and* a sign of sodomy"— thereby historicizing how queer subjects were produced through a shift in sex-gender practices.

While it is impossible to catalog here, it is worth noting the range of historical work that exploded in the late twentieth century that we might or might not call queer now. George Chauncey's bestselling *Gay New York* (1995) proclaimed its subject in the title and offered both a genealogy and a cultural history of queer as a social identity in the US context. Both his book and the raft of scholarly work on gay, lesbian, queer, and trans histories have, through their accumulated empirical weight and critical power, shifted queer from a term of "accusation, pathologization and insult," as Judith Butler put it, to an interpretive framework for thinking with and against gender history. As in other fields of scholarship, the blockbusters that opened the terrain up can obscure earlier tendrils. Carroll Smith-Rosenberg's essay "The Female World of Love and Ritual," which posited that there was a continuum of same-sex relationships to be found in nineteenth-century women's friendships in white middle-class New England, was first published in 1975 but gained its real reputation when it was republished in her 1985 book, *Disorderly Conduct*.

Smith-Rosenberg's work was recuperative of a certain kind of women's history, but it was also prescient about denaturalizing deviance and decoupling the eroticism of female friendships from a progressive narrative march toward marriage and gendered norms of respectability. Nor were all the queer histories unselfconsciously modern. And the predominance of the modern story should not eclipse the way that medievalists and early modernists in particular were among the most important voices of queer critique and method. A literary scholar by training, Carolyn Dinshaw has been hugely influential in defining queer historical thinking. As she wrote in the introduction to her 1999 book, *Getting Medieval*, "I follow what I call a queer historical impulse, an impulse toward making connections across time between, on the one hand, lives, texts, and other cultural phenomena left out of sexual categories back then and, on the other, those left out of current sexual categories now."

That insistence on the radical connections, if not continuities, between past and present resonates with the tenets established in the founding of *Gender and History* in 1989. Of particular relevance for historians, it reminds us that to do queer history is to attend to that space of radical possibility between what history is assigned to do and what history might actually accomplish. It also means working to materialize, as Anjali Arondekar has shown, how archives themselves both reveal and occlude queer histories of gender. What Tim Dean has said about sexuality—"one need not be a strict Freudian to grasp how sex is not primarily an expression of identity but its undoing"—might also be said of gender. His observation might equally be read as a form of queer critique of gender history itself.

Dinshaw was a cofounder, with David Halperin, of a new journal in 1993: *Gay and Lesbian Quarterly* (*GLQ*). An example of the limits of surface reading, *GLQ* was, from its first issues, committedly queer, even as it was at pains to navigate the tensions therein. "We have used the terms 'lesbian' and 'gay,'" they wrote, "in order to foreground what is specifically sexual about the subject matter of *GLQ*. With these words, we want to combat the...ultimately hostile process whereby 'lesbian and gay studies' gets redescribed as 'gender studies'...in order to domesticate it or to make it more academically palatable." The volatile climate of the time, they argued, made naming and claiming lesbian and gay studies as a site for the analysis of all forms of sexuality imperative.

If these are symptoms of social and cultural conflict refracted through the title of the journal, the Q in *GLQ* was no less a psychic seam, aiming to straddle the academic "quarterly" and the "fractious, disruptive...bitchy *queer*." Having opened by declaring it was time for a new journal, Dinshaw and Halperin closed their first editorial by putting a few more stakes into the ground: "[W]e're seeking out in particular new research into historical periods before the twentieth century, into non-Anglophone cultures, and into the experiences of those whose race, ethnicity, age, social class, or sexual practice has detached them from dominant cultures." Those commitments remind us that even if less "domesticated" than gender history, LGBTQ studies faced many of the same issues—intersectionality, Eurocentrism, a modernist bias—as the field of gender history did.

What is the historical relationship of transgender history to this tense and tender kinship between queer critique and gender history? In terms of their emergence as academic fields, they are for all intents and purposes chronologically coeval. This is not to conflate them or to flatten out their specific origin stories. More granular histories would parse those details for as rich and complex a chronology as possible, one that accounts for their points of convergence and divergence over their trajectories as fields of study. But this is not the same as noting their shared historicity: the fact that they came into print in the wake of 1989, borne of much earlier currents and stirrings, to be sure, but taking shape as academic practices in roughly the same historical moment. Rather than via a serial unfolding, gender history, queer history, and transgender history came into view in institutions of higher education in the West at the same general historical moment. Despite the differences and perhaps even frictions and resentments between them, they should be understood as a configuration, a constellation: an assemblage with overlapping formations uncoordinated but operating in shared historical conditions.

Although *TSQ: Transgender Studies Quarterly* was not founded until 2014, there was a field long before there was a dedicated journal. Recalling a conference at the Graduate Center of the City University of New York in 1995, the scholar-activist Susan Stryker recounted the list of session topics ("molly-houses, passionate female friendships, butch-femme dyads, and the Southeast Asian gay diaspora") and observed that the recent wave of transgender scholarship was part of a broader and deeper queer intellectual movement that went back decades. What Stryker was unhappy about was the lack of transgender speakers, wondering why the "entire discussion of 'gender diversity' was subsumed within a discussion of sexual desire—as if the only reason to express gender was to signal the mode of one's attractions and availabilities to potential sex partners?"

Stryker's account of the historical origins of transgender studies in the United States and the United Kingdom emphasized its activist roots (in the group Transgender Nation) and its ongoing dialogue with other "socially engaged" academic fields such as disability studies or critical race theory concerned with how difference is embodied. Stryker cited Sojourner Truth's "Ar'n't I a Woman" speech, drawing express parallels between the insufficiency of the category of "woman" because of its associations with the exclusionary practices of white feminism and the potential of queer studies to obscure intersectionality and perpetuate inequality.

The familiarity of this claim about the failure of unifying categories will be striking for those who recall Sojourner Truth's sensational role in the debut issue of *Gender and History* in 1989. Marta Vicente's question in 2021 in *TGS Quarterly*, "Transgender: A Useful Category?," is also quite familiar. These citations are perhaps merely instances of academic self-referencing. But they also point to the way that shared historicity produced shared vocabularies, repertoires, and (by the twenty-first century) historiographical touchpoints across the fields of gender history, queer theory, and transgender studies—some iconic, others more remarkable for their regular everyday lives. Emily Skidmore's 2017 study, *True Sex: The Lives of Trans Men at the Turn of the 20th Century*, is at pains to argue that trans figures such as Frank Dubois of 1880s Waupun, Wisconsin, sought to pass as conventional men and lead ordinary, unexceptional existences. In spite of this desire, Frank ended up making history: he has the

7. The costume of this participant in the 2017 Trans Day of Action rally in Greenwich Village, New York, speaks to importance of US history in framing trans rights, from Stonewall (1969) to the present. It also locates the trans social movement in the same era as the civil rights and women's liberation movements.

distinction of being the last person to be referred to as a "female husband" in the national US mainstream press.

Whether husbands or not, not all trans people hoping for ordinary lives found it easy to pass. In the course of her dissertation research on the Memphis riots of 1866, for example, the historian Hannah Rosen found the congressional hearing testimony of Frances Thompson and Lucy Smith, who, like a number of formerly enslaved women, had been raped by white men in the course of the city's convulsive violence. Ten years later Thompson was arrested for being a man and wearing women's clothing, allowing southern lawmakers to argue that her claims of rape—which were deemed "pretended outrages"—were a lie. "What can we make of the fact that Thompson—with a woman's identity and a male body—testified that she had been raped during the Memphis riot?" Rosen asks in her 1999 essay about race, gender, and sexual violence in the post–Civil War South. "Was she drawing on Lucy Smith's experience of rape to perform for the committee that she too was a woman? Or had she in fact been raped? Had the rioters been shocked when they discovered the 'truth' about her anatomy? Or were they aware in advance that she was anatomically male? Did they attack her because of that fact? Was the materiality of bodies irrelevant, superseded by a 'script' of black women's sexual wantonness that mattered most?"

Ultimately, Rosen finds, the archive is silent on these questions. What did follow was a campaign of vilification against Thompson in the conservative press, showing with particularly painful vividness how discourses of gender and sexuality played a defining role in political struggles over race—and how transgender histories may be instrumental to their outcomes.

As C. Riley Snorton argues in his study of the racial history of trans identity, to index gender in trans history you must "see racialized gender." So tightly bound are those ways of being that Snorton suggests that to feel Black in the diaspora might be a kind of trans experience. Taken together, Rosen and Snorton are doing the historical work to support what Roderick Ferguson calls "multidimensional queer politics." Scholars taking up the challenges of both queer and transgender history insist, as well, that we must look beyond the confines of the West, and especially of the United States, to resist reproducing the cultural assumptions and methodological biases baked into North American vantage points. T. J. Tallie meets this challenge in his study of white settlement in nineteenth-century South Africa, *Queering Colonial Natal*, when he shows that despite the colonial state's efforts to claim otherwise, African men and women did not consider polygamy and *ilobolo* (bride wealth) aberrant. Indeed, in Indigenous terms they were utterly commonplace, which makes English marriage practices the true queer ones, in the sense of being at odds with their assignment.

And yet it is useful to be reminded of how unquestioned the equation of queer with US-centric experiences can be. A quick Google search of queer history yields two telling results. One is "The Queer History Book List" curated by Penguin Random House, which scarcely touches any subject outside the modern United States. The other is the Organization of American Historians' "Queer History" page, which is a very handy narrative of the subject, and which passes for a universal, if potted, account of the subject. To be clear: the latter is a synthesis of US-based queer narratives in a US-based professional organization dedicated to American history. What is startling is the insularity of the story and the lack of a sense of an "outside" to the categories under question. It references race as Blackness, but again, these are US-based categories, and it does not explore intersectionality beyond African American history.

But a wide world of both gender and queer history is available, as Afsaneh Najmabadi shows in her queer reading of the work of gender in Iranian modernity in her 2005 book *Women with Moustaches and Men without Beards*. In addition to

8. This "amorous couple" from the early nineteenth century graces the cover of Afsaneh Najmabadi's book, *Women with Mustaches, Men Without Beards* (2006), helping us visualize the fluidity of gender roles and systems in modern Iran—and to rethink the centrality of the gender binary in Western histories.

provincializing gender as a category of historical analysis, Najmabadi uses the so-called manliness of the beard to disrupt any easy identification between the sexed body and the performance of gender identity, offering a queer reading dependent on vernacular idiom and Islamic points of reference. "An adult man who shaved his beard was thought to be declaring his desire to be desired by other men," Najmabadi writes. In social terms, beardless men were largely considered "abject characters" and were subject to religious disapproval and sometimes severe punishment.

In some Muslim societies, however, "social practices accommodated such figures through gender cross-dressing and integration in the margins of the world of women, and/or into professions such as music, dancing, and reciting poetry—another reason that sometimes they have been considered effeminate." Yet *khanith* (denoting a person assigned male at birth but using female gender expression) could be read as an intermediate category rather than part of a binary system, suggesting the existence of a continuum between very feminine women and very masculine men.

In Najmabadi's hands, we get a reading of *khanith* that practices gender history, queer theory, and transgender studies all at once, showing how they can riff off each other even as the categories they rely on are distinctive. More specifically, she answers Stryker's call for a mode of reading that "makes visible the normative linkages we generally assume to exist between the biological specificity of the sexually differentiated human body..., and the cultural mechanisms that work to sustain or thwart specific configurations of gendered personhood." Najmabadi does so in part by naming "the cultural mechanism," *khanith*, in order to show up the space(s) between gender that is assigned and gender that is performed. It is a practically perfectly queer reading of a transgender subject in the making.

Historians working on Asia have long been keen to call out the Western hegemonic potential of gender history practices, especially those that are US-centric. As Howard Chiang observed in the introduction to his 2012 collection, *Transgender China*, while scholars and activists debate the relationships among gender, queer and trans studies, and history in the West, "the reconfiguring of our analytical prism with a focus on China would invariably complicate the politics of queer representation and its underlying ideological and social agenda, as well as the practical and political implications." Taking Chiang's cue, the *Journal of Asian Studies* sponsored a forum on Butler's *Gender Trouble* thirty years on, and it featured a number of important critiques. Gail Hershatter acknowledged that Butler helped historians appreciate that "coherent gender is an arduous achievement" through repetition and performance.

But Tamara Loos, a Southeast Asianist, noted that "Butler's gender theory rests upon (even as it critiques) a binary framework (masculine/feminine, male/female, hetero-/homosexual) that does not fit seamlessly in Southeast Asian contexts, where transgender figures historically had a third and ontologically distinct status." Her point is that a binary framework can give the impression that transgender figures were anomalous rather than commonplace in Southeast Asia. What is evident, too, in this context is that the very meanings of common terms—sex, gender, and sexuality—operate differently in communities beyond the United States and Europe. Loos went so far as to argue that because gender is a foreign term in every language other than English, "gender theory has a problem of translation at the core of its project."

Butler's response was frank and to the point. She conceded that she could no longer see translation "as a secondary act." In fact, she wrote, "the category of gender is unthinkable without translation." And she conceded that "those working in Euro-American frameworks have assumed that whatever is said about gender is true if it is conceptually clear within those vocabularies and grammars. If a theory of gender seeks to be generalizable, then it has to pass through translation. And when it takes that passage, the very concept of gender changes—or fails—by virtue of the inflections and usages that are part of other idioms and languages." Hence, she concludes, "there can be no theory of gender without translation, and translation is the condition for a global understanding of gender and a differentiated sense of gender studies. Few tasks are more important for gender research than the critique of monolingualism and authorial control within English."

Significantly for the entwined fields of gender, queer history, and transgender history, Butler also cautioned against universalizing the nonbinary, which sounds like a warning against the triumphalism of that category. In her caution we hear an echo, too, of long-standing worries about the dangers of allowing any one category of analysis to predominate in our research, writing, and teaching about the histories that gender has made and remade—and the genders that history has made and remade as well. Given the ongoing seductions of the liberal progressive narrative, even (and perhaps especially) in times of rightward peril, it seems wise to see the connections between those ongoing concerns and the preoccupations of the present as a clear, but crooked, line.

# Conclusion: Toward the futures of gender history

Rumors about the demise of gender history may be premature. Anxieties about the end of women's history—which have generated commentary and roundtables and even conferences over the last twenty years—are also questionable, in part because the subjects of "women and gender" remain yoked in department titles, undergraduate majors, and PhD preliminary fields. What is researched and taught in the early 2020s reflects this entanglement, as well as the scope of what now counts as the right and proper subjects of these histories. At the University of North Carolina, for example, courses cover the world and include the history of family, work, and welfare; the history of women's movements; the gendered history of the nation, race, and ethnicities; the history of colonialism; the history of masculinity, the history of sexuality; the history of violence, the military, and war and peace; and the gendered history of popular culture and collective memory. Among the themes of the undergraduate concentration are "the struggles for equal rights of women in the economy, politics, society and the family, as well as the complex constructions of gender norms and images, and their consequences for all aspects of political, social, and cultural life."

Sharon Block's careful data mining reveals that in 1985, "gender" occurred less than once in every 10,000 words in abstracts—and that by 2005, that had increased eightfold. Thirty years after the founding of *Gender and History*, gender history shows up everywhere, threaded through all manner of topics and structuring strong commitments to intersectional research and teaching. And its impact continues to be felt on the choice of subject and methodological approach equally. In their 2017 book *Reproductive Justice*, Loretta Ross and Rickie Solinger acknowledge the work that the field has done to query the fixity of binaries in ways that require critical attention even when gender per se is not the focus. "This book recognizes the limits of traditional, biologically based binary definitions of gender," they emphasize, "at the same time that it chronicles and analyzes histories that these definitions have produced." They join a cohort of scholars drawing attention to the fact that at this moment in the history of women and gender, those very categories are in flux, challenged by queer and trans subjects and practitioners in ways that compel readers to take notice so that they remain mindful of the ways that historical referents are steeped in a two-gender system at odds with how many people have lived their lives.

And yet there is perhaps little cause to be sanguine. While the leading lights of gender history surfaced in this book (Joan Scott, Afsaneh Najmabadi, Jennifer Morgan) have tended to be at US elite private institutions, the critical mass of scholarship in the field has been produced in public universities and liberal arts colleges that have been in fiscal crisis for at least two decades. With respect to such a crisis, there is no end in sight, not least because of the unprecedented toll that the global pandemic has taken on higher education and its student, staff, and faculty communities. Of the three dozen historians of gender surveyed for this *VSI* project, some were confident that gender history was embedded in the discipline, but the majority referenced the 1990s as the high-water mark for the field *qua* field. The fact that, as one respondent put it, "gender history is both more influential and less easily identifiable as time goes on" was more alarming than comforting to most. Beyond the arena of higher education, the story may be one of stasis at best. As the teacher Bridget Riley of

Stone Middle School observed in 2022, "despite the push to remedy gender imbalance in social studies . . . textbooks, as well as an understanding of the negative impacts of a curriculum that is not representative of a diverse student body, change has been slow."

What's more, in an ongoing climate of open hostility to critical race theory and trans/gender/queer thinking—hostility that weaponizes difference and authorizes violence against those who appear to embody it across a range of identities—the global attack on gender studies, and with it gender history, is real. In 2018 the Hungarian government banned the MA degree in gender studies. Erzsébet Barát, writing for a 2020 special issue of *Baltic Worlds*, traces what she calls the discreditation of gender through the culture wars in defense of the Hungarian people—part of an accelerating right-wing populist discourse that labeled feminism an alien discourse. In the United States, women's and gender studies and ethnic studies programs, together with faculty in humanities departments like history, are increasingly first on the chopping block, while legal access to abortion is in the sights of activists determined not just to rewrite but to retake the history of women and gender for a far-right agenda. Progress is not simply precarious. It is simply inadequate to the task of understanding what work gender history, in all its complexities and limitations, has done and remains poised to do in the world.

That work is unfinished, and not only because of backlash against "gains" in either the field or in the social and political landscape at large. There's no denying that there have been important shifts and changes through the very accumulation of the work of gender history and its visibility in the academy and beyond. Gender history speaks to everything from war to the economy to colonialism, from race to technology to poverty to memory, from work to community to nation, from struggle to resilience, and from joy to sorrow and rage. Though by one definition it is a field of scholarship, gender history is also ever-present in daily life—that is to say, it is happening, and being told and retold, all around us. That many (if not all) who think about it expect, even desire, a progressive narrative for gender history is instructive. It reminds us of how embedded the field itself has been in the specific historical events and experiences that generated the Western democratic liberal order and its powerful progressive imaginaries—imaginaries that acknowledge race and sexual difference, for example, but do not always act as if they are foundational to progressive futures.

This is not to suggest that transformations have not happened, for they surely have. I prefer the metaphor of the relay or the exchange across fields to the arc of progress, in part because those feel less charged by assumptions of white liberal individualism and saviorism. In any case, even a very short introduction, one that historicizes gender history's formations and interlocutors and represents it as part of the recent past, can point to the space between the role it has been assigned and the work it is capable of doing. If this is a kind of queer project for gender history, it is one which acknowledges that binaries are at once fragmented and persistent, that intersectional practice is an aspiration requiring urgent attention, and that gender as a category of historical analysis is itself produced by imperial ways of thinking and doing, both inherited and at work in the present.

If we want to signal that gender history is not just a field or a subject but a critical methodology, we are obliged to take these exhortations seriously. As a feminist scholar of empire invested in strategies that attend to disruptive histories from below, I submit that we need to regularly renew our commitments to decolonizing gender history. That means, of course, materializing forms of historical gender not readily legible in mainstream histories that fail to account especially for minoritized racial subjects. But it also means remaining alive to how our own practices as gender historians carry more than traces of modern Western thinking and imperial*ized* ways of knowing—and working continuously to unlearn and unsettle what appears normative across time and place.

It means, too, practicing a critical humility when it comes to imagining what history of any stripe can capture, and what it cannot. The increasing visibility of work like Saidiya Hartman's and that of other Black, Brown, and Indigenous history-makers under the rubric of "critical fabulation"—a kind of impossible storytelling, given the limits of archives and other materials considered properly historical—is a promising terrain upon which gender history might test its commitments to addressing what counts as the history of gender. We must press against the seams of the knowable, official archive and speculate responsibly when it comes to writing what we might call gender history against erasure.

Whatever its future, the field of gender history will always be a palimpsest of past and present, working through its own implication in the politics of the here and now and serving as an evolving archive of that exhilarating, unruly project.

# References

## Introduction

Joan Wallach Scott, *Gender and the Politics of History* (New York: Columbia University Press, 1988) [chapter 8 for the Sears case]; and *The Politics of the Veil* (Princeton: Princeton University Press, 2010).

Gloria Wekker, "How Families Navigate Empire," *Sydney Review of Books*, February 21, 2020; Here Wekker talks about reading Carby in the Netherlands in the 1970s.

Sara Salem, "On Transnational Feminist Solidarity: The Case of Angela Davis in Egypt," *Signs* 43, no. 2 (2018): 245–502.

Editorial Collective, "Why Gender and History?" *Gender and History* 1, no. 1 (1989): 2.

## Chapter 1

Tracy L. Snell, "Women in Jail 1989," Bureau of Justice Statistics Special Report, March 1992, https://bjs.ojp.gov/content/pub/pdf/wj89.pdf.

Editorial Collective, "Why Gender and History?" *Gender and History* 1, no. 1 (1989): 1–6

Kathleen Canning, "Feminist History after the Linguistic Turn: Historicizing Discourse and Experience," *Signs* 19, no. 2 (1994): 386–404.

Natalie Zemon Davis, "'Women's History' in Transition: The European Case," *Feminist Studies* 3/4 (1976): 83–103.

Dorothy Sterling, *We Are Your Sisters: Black Women in the Nineteenth Century* (New York: W. W. Norton, 1984), 152–53.

Nell Irvin Painter, *Sojourner Truth: A Life, a Symbol* (New York: W. W. Norton, 1996); and her letter to the editor, "The Truth of the Matter," *New Yorker*, May 23, 2022, 3.

Evelyn Brooks Higginbotham, "Beyond the Sound of Silence: Afro-American Women in History," *Gender and History* 1, no. 1 (Spring 1989): 53, 63.

Aida Hurtado, "Relating to Privilege: Seduction and Rejection in the Subordination of White Women and Women of Color," *Signs* 14, no. 2 (1989): 833–55.

Joanne Meyerowitz, *How Sex Changed: A History of Transsexuality in the United States* (Cambridge, MA: Harvard University Press, 2004), 115.

Judith Lorber, "From the Editor," *Gender and Society* 1, no. 2 (1987): 123.

Nancy Hartsock, "Postmodernism and Political Change: Issues for Feminist Theory," *Cultural Critique* 14 (1989–90): 21.

Joanne Meyerowitz, "A History of 'Gender,'" *American Historical Review* 113, no. 5 (2008): 1346–56.

Dorothy Ko, "Gender," in *A Concise Companion to History*, ed. Ulinka Rublack (Oxford: Oxford University Press, 2011), 224.

Carol Karlsen, *Devil in the Shape of a Woman* (New York: W.W. Norton, 1987)

Joan Scott, "History in Crisis? The Others' Side of the Story," *American Historical Review* 94, no. 3 (1989): 680–92.

Dyan Elliot, "The Three Ages of Joan Scott," *American Historical Review* 113, no. 5 (2008): 1390–1403.

Heidi Tinsman, "A Paradigm of Our Own: Joan Scott in Latin American History," *American Historical Review* 113, no. 5 (2009): 1357–74.

Amanda Vickery, "Golden Age to Separate Spheres? A Review of the Categories and Chronology of English Women's History," *Historical Journal* 36, no. 2 (1993): 383–41.

Antoinette Burton, "Catherine Hall," Bloomsbury History: Theory and Method (London: Bloomsbury, 2020), http://dx.doi.org/10.5040/9781350970816.020.

Jane Rendall and Keith McClelland, "Leonore Davidoff and the Founding of Gender & History," *Gender History* 28, no. 2 (2016): 28.

Denise Riley "Does a Sex Have a History?" *New Formations* 1 (1987): 35–46. Quote is p. 38.

Gayatri Spivak, "The Rani of Sirmur: An Essay in Reading the Archives," *History and Theory* 24, no. 3 (1985): 257–72; and "Three Women's Texts and a Critique of Imperialism" *Critical Inquiry* 12, no. 1 (1985): 243–61.

Elsa Barkley Brown, "Polyrhythms and Improvization: Lessons for Women's History," *History Workshop Journal* 31 (1991): 85–90.

Angela Davis, *Women, Race and Class* (New York: Random House, 1981).

Rafia Zakaria, *Against White Feminism: Notes on Disruption* (New York: W. W. Norton, 2021).

## Chapter 2

Angela Woollacott, *On Her Their Lives Depend: Munitions Workers in the Great War* (Berkeley: University of California Press, 1994).

Elena Shulman, *Stalinism on the Frontier of Empire: Women and State Formation in the Soviet Far East* (Cambridge: Cambridge University Press, 2012).

Leila Ahmed, "Women and the Advent of Islam," *Signs* 11, no. 4 (1986): 665, 668.

Leila Ahmed, *Gender and Women in Islam* (New Haven, CT: Yale University Press, 1992), 2.

Clare Midgley, *Women against Slavery: The British Campaigns, 1780–1870* (London: Routledge, 1992), 5.

Kristin Hoganson, *Fighting for American Manhood: How Gender Politics Provoked the Spanish-American and Philippine-American Wars* (New Haven, CT: Yale University Press, 1998), 4.

Londa Schiebinger, *Nature's Body: Gender in the Making of Modern Science* (New Brunswick, NJ: Rutgers University Press, 1995), x, xiii.

Joan B. Landes, *Visualizing the Nation: Gender, Representation, and Revolution in Eighteenth-Century France* (Ithaca, NY: Cornell University Press, 2003).

Clare Crowston, *Fabricating Women: The Seamstresses of Old Regime France* (Durham, NC: Duke University Press, 2001), 2, 7.

Suzanne Desan, "Recent Historiography on the French Revolution and Gender," *Journal of Social History* 52, no. 3 (2019).

Laura Frader, *Breadwinners and Citizens: Gender in the Making of the French Social Model* (Durham, NC: Duke University Press, 2008).

Elizabeth Colwill, "Freedwomen's Familial Politics: Marriage, War and Rites of Registry in Post-Emancipation Saint-Domingue," in *Gender, War, and Politics: Transatlantic Perspectives, 1775–1830,* ed. Karen Hagemann, Gisela Mettele, and Jane Rendall (Basingstoke, UK: Palgrave Macmillan, 2010), 71–89.

Gail Hershatter, "Disquiet in the House of Gender," *Journal of Asian Studies* 71, no. 4 (2012): 891.

Sarah Chambers, *From Subjects to Citizens: Honor, Gender, and Politics in Arequipa, Peru, 1780–1854* (University Park: Pennsylvania State University Press, 1999), 5.

Sueann Caufield, *In Defense of Honor: Sexual Morality, Modernity, and Nation in Early Twentieth-Century Brazil* (Durham, NC: Duke University Press, 2000), 4.

Tamara Walker, "That Is How Whores Get Punished: Gender, Race, and the Culture of Honor-Based Violence in Colonial Latin America," *Journal of Women's History* 31, no. 2 (2019): 11–22.

Jean Allman, "Rounding Up Spinsters: Gender Chaos and Unmarried Women in Colonial Asante," *Journal of African History* 37, no. 2 (1996): 207.

Teresa A. Barnes, *"We Women Worked So Hard": Gender, Urbanization, and Social Reproduction in Colonial Harare, Zimbabwe, 1930–1956* (Portsmouth, NH: Heinemann, 1999).

Kathy Skidmore-Hess, "Review," *National Women's Studies Association Journal* 14, no. 2 (2002): 238.

David Maxwell, "Review," *American Historical Review* 106, no. 5 (2001): 1913.

Rob Morrell, "Of Boys and Men: Masculinity and Gender in Southern African Studies," in "Masculinities in Southern Africa," special issue, *Journal of Southern African Studies* 24, no. 4 (1998): 605.

Lisa Lindsay and Stefan Meischer, eds., *Men and Masculinities in Modern Africa* (Portsmouth, NH: Heinemann, 2003).

John Tosh, *Manliness and Masculinities in Nineteenth-Century Britain* (London: Routledge, 1993), 115.

Kathleen Brown, *Good Wives, Nasty Wenches, and Anxious Patriarchs: Gender, Race, and Power in Colonial Virginia* (Chapel Hill: University of North Carolina Press, 1996), 5–6.

Irene Silverblatt, *Moon, Sun, and Witches: Gender Ideologies and Class in Inca and Colonial Peru* (Princeton: Princeton University Press, 1987).

Merry Weisner-Hanks, ed., *Gendered Temporalities in the Early Modern World* (Amsterdam: Amsterdam University Press, 2018).

Alexandra Shepard and Garthine Walker, "Gender, Change and Periodisation," *Gender and History* 20, no. 3 (Fall 2008): 453–62.

Antoinette Burton. "A 'Pilgrim Reformer' at the Heart of the Empire: Behramji Malabari in Late-Victorian London," *Gender and History* 8, no. 2 (1996): 175–96.

Mrinalini Sinha, *Colonial Masculinity: The "Manly Englishman" and the "Effeminate Bengali" in the Late Nineteenth Century* (Manchester, UK: Manchester University Press, 1995).

Darlene Clark Hine and Earnestine Jenkins, eds., *A Question of Manhood: A Reader in U.S. Black Men's History and Masculinity*, vol. 1 (Bloomington: Indiana University Press, 1999), xii, xvii.

Laura Engelstein, *The Keys to Happiness: Sex and the Search for Modernity in Fin-de-Siècle Russia* (Ithaca, NY: Cornell University Press, 1992).

Pete Sigal, *From Moon Goddesses to Virgins* (Austin: University of Texas Press, 2000); and *The Flower and the Scorpion* (Durham, NC: Duke University Press, 2011).

Judith Walkowitz, *Prostitution and Victorian Society* (Cambridge: Cambridge University Press, 1980).

Anna Clark, *Desire: A History of European Sexuality* (London: Routledge, 2019), 2.

Joan Scott, "Reflections on Women and Gender in Twentieth-Century Mexico: Introduction," *Gender and History* 20, no. 1 (Spring 2008): 150.

Denise Riley, "Does Sex Have a History? 'Women' and Feminism," *New Formations* 1 (1987): 35–46.

Cornelia Drayton and Lisa Levenstein, "The Big Tent of U.S. Women's and Gender History: A State of the Field," *Journal of American History* 99, no. 3 (2021): 793–817.

Kevin P. Murphy and Jennifer M. Spear, "Historicizing Sexuality and Gender," *Gender and History* 22, no. 3 (2010): 527–37.

## Chapter 3

Nancy L. Green, "Changing Paradigms in Migration Studies: From Men to Women to Gender," *Gender and History* 24, no. 3 (2012): 782–98.

Nell Irvin Painter, "A Prize-Winning Book Revisited," *Journal of Women's History* 2, no. 3 (1991): 132.

Susan Cahn, "Women Defining and Defying the Color Line," *Journal of Women's History* 17, no. 3 (2005): 169.

Sonya O. Rose, "Gender History/Women's History: Is Feminist Scholarship Losing Its Critical Edge?" *Journal of Women's History* 5, no. 1 (1993): 89.

Kimberlé Crenshaw, "Demarginalizing the Intersection of Race and Sex: A Black Feminist Critique of Antidiscrimination Doctrine, Feminist Theory and Antiracist Politics," *University of Chicago Legal Forum* 1, Article 8 (1989): 139–67.

Stuart Hall, "Race, The Floating Signifier," 1997; transcript of the talk: https://www.mediaed.org/transcripts/Stuart-Hall-Race-the-Floating-Signifier-Transcript.pdf.

Eileen Boris, "Gender, Race, and Rights: Listening to Critical Race Theory," *Journal of Women's History* 6, no. 2 (1994): 111.

Rosalind Rosenberg, "The Conjuncture of Race and Gender," *Journal of Women's History* 14, no. 2 (2002): 71.

Jean Allman and Antoinette Burton, "Editors' Note," *Journal of Women's History* 19, no. 2 (2007): 7.

Michele Mitchell, "Silences Broken, Silences Kept: Gender and Sexuality in African-American History," *Gender and History* 11, no. 3 (1999): 433–44.

Brenda Child, *Boarding School Seasons: American Indian Families, 1900–1940* (Lincoln: University of Nebraska Press, 1998).

J. Kehaulani Kauanui, *Paradoxes of Hawaiian Sovereignty Land, Sex, and the Colonial Politics of State Nationalism* (Durham, NC: Duke University Press, 2018).

Evelyn Blackwood, "Sexuality and Gender in Certain Native American Tribes: The Case of Cross-Gender Females", *Signs* 10, no. 1 (184): 27–42.

Nancy Shoemaker, "Native-American Women in History," *OAH Magazine of History* 9, no. 4 (1995): 10–14.

Joanne Woodsun, "Gender and Sexuality in Native American Societies: A Bibliography," *American Indian Quarterly* 19, no. 4 (1995): 527–55.

Luana Ross, "Race, Gender, and Social Control: Voices of Imprisoned Native American and White Women," *Wicazo Sa Review* 10, no. 2 (1994): 17–39.

Joy James, "Gender, Race, and Radicalism: Teaching the Autobiographies of Native and African American Women Activists," *Feminist Teacher* 8, no. 3 (1994): 129–39.

Gender History

Ashley Glassburn Faletti, "Archival Absence: The Burden of History," *Settler Colonial Studies* 5, no. 2 (2015): 128–44.

Tadashi Dozono, "Teaching Alternative and Indigenous Gender Systems in World History: A Queer Approach," *History Teacher* 50, no. 3 (2017): 425–26.

Deborah Gray White, *Ar'n't I a Woman? Female Slaves in the Plantation South* (New York: W. W. Norton, 1985), 13.

Carolyn See, "History of Female Slaves in the South Is Revised," *Los Angeles Review of Books*, January 7, 1986, https://www.latimes.com/archives/la-xpm-1986-01-07-vw-14085-story.html.

Darlene Clark Hine, "*Ar'n't I a Woman?: Female Slaves in the Plantation South*: Twenty Years After," *Journal of African American History* 92, no. 1 (2007): 13–21.

Jennifer L. Morgan, *Laboring Women: Reproduction and Gender in New World Slavery* (Philadelphia: University of Pennsylvania Press, 2004), 6.

Maris Fuentes, *Dispossessed Lives: Enslaved Women, Violence, and the Archive* (Philadelphia: University of Pennsylvania Press, 2018), 44.

Review of *Unequal Sisters: A Multicultural Reader in U.S. Women's History*, by Vicki Ruiz and Ellen DuBois, *Journal of Women's History* 3, no. 1 (1991): 139–40.

Bernice McNair, "Angela Davis and *Women, Race, & Class*: A Pioneer in Integrative RGC Studies," *Race, Gender & Class*, 10, no. 3 (2003): 9–22.

Siobhan Somerville, *Queering the Color Line: Race and the Invention of Homosexuality in American Culture* (Durham, NC: Duke University Press, 2000), 4–5.

Nayan Shah, *Stranger Intimacy: Contesting Race, Sexuality and the Law in the North American West* (Berkeley: University of California Press, 2012), 28.

Julia Camacho, Review of *Stranger Intimacy: Contesting Race, Sexuality and the Law in the North American West*, by Nayan Shah, H-Borderlands, H-Net Reviews, February, 2013, http://www.h-net.org/reviews/showrev.php?id=35247.

Paul Gilroy, *The Black Atlantic* (Cambridge, MA: Harvard University Press, 1993), 85.

Alison Parker, "Intersecting Histories of Gender, Race, and Disability," *Journal of Women's History* 27, no. 1 (2015): 178.

Niall Ferguson et al., eds., *The Shock of the Global: The 1970s in Perspective* (Cambridge, MA: Harvard University Press, 2010).

Wilson Chacko Jacob, *Working Out Egypt: Effendi Masculinity and Subject Formation in Colonial Modernity, 1870–1940* (Durham, NC: Duke University Press, 2011).

Angela Wanhalla, *Matters of the Heart: A History of Interracial Marriage on New Zealand* (Auckland: Auckland University Press, 2014).

Carina Ray, *Crossing the Color Line: Race, Sex, and the Contested Politics of Colonialism in Ghana* (Athens: Ohio University Press, 2015).

Michele Mitchell, "Turns of the Kaleidoscope: 'Race,' Ethnicity, and Analytical Patterns in American Women's and Gender History," *Journal of Women's History* 25, no. 4 (2013): 46–73.

## Chapter 4

Karen Hagemann and Maria Teresa Fernández-Aceves, "Gendering Trans/National Historiographies: Similarities and Differences in Comparison," *Journal of Women's History* 19, no. 1 (2007): 151.

Adele Perry, "Gender Goes Global: The Writing of Transnational Histories," *Journal of Women's History* 21, no. 2 (Summer 2009): 138–45.

Adrienne Rich, *An Atlas of the Difficult World: Poems, 1988–1991* (New York: W. W. Norton, 1991), 6.

Marilyn Booth, "Guest Editorial Note: Women's Autobiography in South Asia and the Middle East," *Journal of Women's History* 25, no. 2 (2013): 8.

*AHR* Roundtable Introduction, "Historians and the Question of 'Modernity,'" *American Historical Review* 116, no. 3 (June 2011): 631.

Carol Symes, "When We Talk about Modernity," *American Historical Review* 116, no. 3 (June 2011): 717.

Peter N. Stearns, *Gender in World History* (London: Routledge, 2000), "Introduction" and Part I.

Sarah B. Pomeroy, *Goddesses, Whores, Wives, and Slaves: Women in Classical Antiquity* (London: Pimlico, 1975).

Scott Rubarth, "Competing Constructions of Masculinity In Ancient Greece," *Athens Journal of Humanities & Arts* 1, no. 1 (2014): 21–32.

Brooke Holmes, *Gender: Antiquity and Its Legacies* (London: I.B. Tauris, 2012), 51.

Gender History

Allison Surtees and Jennifer Dyer, eds., *Exploring Gender Diversity in the Ancient World* (Edinburgh: Edinburgh University Press, 2022).

Susan Kingsley Kent, *Gender: A World History* (Oxford: Oxford University Press, 2021), 25–26.

Merry Weisner-Hanks, ed., *Gendered Temporalities in the Early Modern World* (Amsterdam: Amsterdam University Press, 2018); and her *The Marvelous Hairy Girls* (New Haven, CT: Yale University Press, 2009).

Ulrike Strasser and Heidi Tinsman, "Engendering World History," *Radical History Review* 91 (2005): 151.

Merry Wiesner-Hanks, "Introduction," in *Gendered Temporalities in the Early Modern World* (Amsterdam: Amsterdam University Press, 2018), 7–16.

Oyèrónké Oyěwùmí, *The Invention of Women: Making an African Sense of Western Gender Discourses* (Minneapolis: University of Minnesota Press, 1997), ix.

Kathrine Binhammer, "Is the Eighteenth Century a Colonizing Temporality?" *Eighteenth Century Fiction* 33, no. 2 (2020–21): 199–204.

Stephen O. Murray, "On Subordinating Native American Cosmologies to the Empire of Gender," *Current Anthropology* 35, no. 1 (1994): 59–61.

Afsaneh Najmabadi, *Women with Mustaches and Men without Beards: Gender and Sexual Anxieties of Iranian Modernity* (Berkeley: University of California Press, 2005), 3–4.

Maria Lugones, "The Coloniality of Gender," *Worlds and Knowledges Otherwise* 2, no. 2 (Spring 2008): 1–17.

Nancy Rose Hunt, "Placing African Women's History and Locating Gender," *Social History* 14, no. 3 (1989): 363, 373.

Mutiat Titilope Oladejo, "Female Historians and Knowledge Production for Women's Studies: The Nigerian Example since 1974," *International Journal of Gender and Women's Studies* 6, no. 1 (2018): 30–37.

Jean Allman, "Academic Reparation and Stepping Aside," *Africa Is a Country* (2020), https://africasacountry.com/2020/11/academic-reparation-and-stepping-aside.

Catherine Cole, Takyiwaa Manu, and Stephan Miescher, eds., *Africa After Gender?* (Bloomington: Indiana University Press, 2007), 1–11.

Antoinette Burton, "Parsing the Woman Question, Rethinking Feminist History," *Journal of Women's History* 20, no. 1 (2008): 217.

Elizabeth LaCouture, "Translating Domesticity in Chinese History and Historiography," *American Historical Review* 124, no. 4 (2019): 1278; see also her *Dwelling in the World: Family, House, and Home in Tianjin, China, 1860–1960* (New York: Columbia University Press, 2021).

Tani Barlow, "Asian Perspective," response to "Beyond Dichotomies: Interdependence in Mid-Nineteenth Century Working Class Families in the United States," *Gender and History* 1, no. 3 (Fall 1989): 318–27.

Howard Chiang, ed., *Transgender China* (London: Palgrave Macmillan, 2012), 7.

Mrinalini Sinha, *Specters of Mother India: The Global Restructuring of an Empire* (Durham, NC: Duke University Press, 2006), 55, 54, 153; see also Sinha, "A Global Perspective on Gender: What's South Asia Got to Do with It?," in *South Asian Feminisms*, ed. Ania Loomba and Ritty Lukose (Durham, NC: Duke University Press, 2012), 356–74.

Tanika Sarkar, *Words to Win: The Making of "Amar Jian," A Modern Autobiography* (Delhi: Kali for Women, 1999).

Mytheli Sreenivas, "Women's and Gender History in Modern India," in *Making Women's Histories: Beyond National Perspectives*, ed. Pamela S. Nadall and Kate Haulman (New York: New York University Press, 2013), 180.

Tanika Sarkar, *Hindu Wife, Hindu Nation: Community, Religion and Cultural Nationalism* (Delhi: Permanent Black, 2003).

Emily Martin, "The Egg and the Sperm: How Science Has Constructed a Romance Based on Stereotypical Male-Female Roles," *Signs*, 16, no. 3 (1991): 498, 501.

## Chapter 5

Judith Butler, *Gender Trouble: Feminism and the Subversion of Identity* (New York: Routledge, 1999), p. viii.

Judith Butler, *Undoing Gender* (New York: Routledge, 2004), 9.

Judith Butler and Joan Scott, eds., *Feminists Theorize the Political* (New York: Routledge, 1992).

Nancy Cott, "What Is Gender History?," speech delivered at the Advanced Placement luncheon at the American Historical Association (Seattle), 2005, https://apcentral.collegeboard.org/courses/ap-united-states-history/classroom-resources/what-is-gender-history.

Dan Healey, "Evgeniia/Evgenii: Queer Case Histories in the First Years of Soviet Power," *Gender and History* 9, no. 1 (1997): 83–106.

Matt Houlbrook, "'Lady Austin's Camp Boys': Constituting the Queer Subject in 1930s London," *Gender & History* 14, no. 1 (2002): 31–61.

George Chauncey, *Gay New York: Gender, Urban Culture, and the Making of the Gay Male World, 1890–1940* (New York: Basic Books, 2005).

Judith Butler, "Critically Queer," *GLQ* 1 (1993): 18.

Carroll Smith-Rosenberg, "The Female World of Love and Ritual: Relations between Women in Nineteenth-Century America," *Signs* 1, no. 1 (1975): 1–29.

Carolyn Dinshaw et al., "Theorizing Queer Temporalities: A Roundtable Discussion," *GLQ* 13, no. 2–3 (2007): 177–95.

Carolyn Dinshaw, *Getting Medieval: Sexualities and Communities, Pre- and Postmodern* (Durham, NC: Duke University Press, 1999), 1.

Anjali Arondekar, *For the Record: On Sexuality and the Colonial Archive in India* (Durham, NC: Duke University Press, 2009).

Tim Dean, "No Sex Please, We're American," *American Literary History* 27, no. 3 (2015): 616.

Carolyn Dinshaw and David M. Halperin, "Editorial," *GLQ* 1 (1993): iii.

Howard Chiang, ed., *Transgender China* (New York: Palgrave Macmillan, 2012).

Susan Stryker, "De/Colonizing Transgender Studies of China," in *Transgender China*, ed. Howard Chiang (New York: Palgrave Macmillan, 2012), 287–92.

Susan Stryker, "(De)Subjugated Knowledges: An Introduction to Transgender Studies," in *The Transgender Studies Reader* (New York: Routledge, 2006),1, 3.

Marta V. Vicente, "Transgender: A Useful Category? Or, How the Historical Study of 'Transsexual' and 'Transvestite' Can Help Us Rethink 'Transgender' as a Category," *TSQ: Transgender Studies Quarterly* 8, no. 4 (2021): 426–42.

Emily Skidmore, *True Sex: The Lives of Trans Men at the Turn of the 20th Century* (New York: New York University Press, 2017), 11.

Jen Manion, *Female Husbands: A Trans History* (Cambridge: Cambridge University Press, 2020).

Hannah Rosen, "'Not That Sort of Women': Race, Gender, and Sexual Violence during the Memphis Riot of 1866," in *Sex, Love, Race:*

*Crossing Boundaries in North American History*, ed. Martha Hodes (New York: New York University Press, 1999), 184–85.

C. Riley Snorton, *Black on Both Sides: A Racial History of Trans Identity* (Minneapolis: University of Minnesota Press, 2017), 8. In fact, the index entry for gender in his book says, "see racialized gender."

Roderick A. Ferguson, *One-Dimensional Queer* (Cambridge: Polity Press, 2019).

T.J. Tallie, *Queering Colonial Natal: Indigeneity and the Violence of Belonging in Southern Africa* (Minneapolis: University of Minnesota Press, 2019). *Ilobolo* is the Zulu ritual cattle exchange between the groom's family and the bride's (p. 10).

The Queer History Book List (https://www.penguinrandomhouse.com/the-read-down/the-queer-history-book-list/) and the Organization of American Historians' "Queer History" page (https://www.oah.org/tah/issues/2019/may/queer-history/).

Afsaneh Najmabadi, *Women with Moustaches and Men without Beards* (Cambridge, MA: Harvard University Press, 2006), p. 17.

Gail Hershatter, "*Gender Trouble*'s Afterlife in Chinese Studies," *Journal of Asian Studies* 79, no. 4 (2020): 913.

Tamara Loos, "Reading *Gender Trouble* in Southeast Asia," *Journal of Asian Studies* 79, no. 4 (2020): 927–46.

Judith Butler, "Reflections on *Gender Trouble* Thirty Years Later: Reply to Hershatter, Loos, and Patel," *Journal of Asian Studies* 79, no. 4 (2020): 975–76.

Ismat Chugtai, *The Crooked Line* (New York: Feminist Press, 2006; originally published 1943).

## Conclusion

Susan Pedersen, "The Future of Feminist History," *Perspectives on History*, October 1, 2000.

Alice Kessler-Harris, "Do We Still Need Women's History?" *Chronicle of Higher Education* 54, no. 15 (December 7, 2007): B6.

"Women and Power: New Questions in the History of Gender," A Roundtable with Professor Susan Pedersen (European Institute, November 2021), https://www.eui.eu/events?id=541434.

Fields of Study, UNC Department of History, https://history.unc.edu/what-we-study/womens-and-gender-history/.

Sharon Block, "What, Where, When and Sometimes Why: Data Mining Women's History Abstracts," *Journal of Women's History* 23, no. 1 (2011): 81–109.

Loretta Ross and Rickie Solinger, *Reproductive Justice* (Berkeley: University of California Press, 2017), 6.

Bridget Riley, "Missing Women: Tackling Gender Imbalance in Social Studies Textooks," *Perspectives on History*, December 8, 2021.

Elizabeth Redden, "Global Attack on Gender Studies," *Inside Higher Ed*, December 5, 2018, https://www.insidehighered.com/news/2018/12/05/gender-studies-scholars-say-field-coming-under-attack-many-countries-around-globe.

Erzsébet Barát, "Stigmatization of Feminism: Gender Studies as 'Gender Ideology' in Rightwing Populist Political Discourse in Hungary," *Baltic Worlds* 13, no. 1 (2020): 21–30.

Kay Neufield, "Nine Faculty Positions Eliminated at UMF Cut from Humanities and Social Sciences," *Sun Journal*, May 7, 2022, https://www.sunjournal.com/2022/05/07/nine-faculty-positions-eliminated-at-umf-cut-from-humanities-and-social-sciences/.

Judith Lorber, *The New Gender Paradox* (Cambridge: Polity Press, 2022).

"Impossible storytelling" is from the Museum of Modern Art's exhibit "Critical Fabulations," https://www.moma.org/calendar/galleries/5378; and Saidiya Hartman, *Wayward Lives, Beautiful Experiments: Intimate Histories of Riotous Black Girls, Troublesome Women, and Queer Radicals* (New York: Norton, 2019), is one example from Hartman's corpus of work.

# Further reading

## Overviews

Susan Kingsley Kent's *Gender: A World History* (Oxford: Oxford University Press, 2020) provides a synthetic, sweeping account rooted in decades of scholarship and a global approach. For those interested specifically in how gender history has been taught, see Ellen Vicki L. Ruiz and Carol DuBois, *Unequal Sisters: A Multicultural Reader in U.S. Women's History* (New York: Routledge, 1990) and Merry Wiesner-Hanks and Urmi Engineer Willoughby, *A Primer for Teaching Women, Gender, and Sexuality in World History* (Durham, NC: Duke University Press, 2018).

Titles that helped define the limits and possibilities of gender history early on include Angela Davis, *Women, Race and Class* (New York: Random House, 1981); Cherríe Moraga and Gloria E. Anzaldúa, eds., *This Bridge Called My Back: Writings by Radical Women of Color* (San Francisco: Aunt Lute, 1983); and Hazel V. Carby, "White Woman Listen! Black Feminism and the Boundaries of Sisterhood," in Heidi Safia Mirza, ed., *Black British Feminism: A Reader* (London: Routledge, 1997).

For work that speaks to the stakes of gender history as a critical practice in a variety of ways, see Bonnie G. Smith, *The Gender of History: Men, Women and Historical Practice* (Cambridge, MA: Harvard University Press, 2000); Laura Lee Downs, *Writing Gender History* (London: Bloomsbury, 2010); Susan Lanser, *The Sexuality of History: Modernity and the Sapphic, 1585–1830* (Chicago: University of Chicago Press, 2014); Marisa Fuentes, *Dispossessed Lives: Enslaved Women, Violence, and the Archive*

(Philadelphia: University of Pennsylvania Press, 2018); Saidiya Hartman, *Wayward Lives, Beautiful Experiments: Intimate Histories of Riotous Black Girls, Troublesome Women, and Queer Radicals* (New York: Norton, 2020); and Rafia Zakaria, *Against White Feminism: Notes on Disruption* (New York: Norton, 2021).

## The beginnings of the field

Academic journals have been and remain foundational to the field. These include *Gender and History* (1989–present); the *Journal of Women's History* (1989–present); the *Journal of the History of Sexuality* (1990–present); *GLQ: A Journal of Lesbian and Gay Studies* (1993–present); and *TSQ: Transgender Studies Quarterly* (2104–present).

Michel Foucault's work—especially *The History of Sexuality*, volume 1 (Paris: Gallimard, 1976)—was influential for the first generation of historians working on gender, as were postcolonial theorists such as Gayatri Spivak, whose ""Three Women's Texts and a Critique of Imperialism" (*Critical Inquiry* 12, no. 1 [1985]: 243–61)" and "Can the Subaltern Speak? (see Rosalind C. Morris, *Can the Subaltern Speak?: Reflections on the History of an* Idea [New York: Columbia University Press, 2010]) offered counter-histories and analogies of use in discussing gender as a category.

Early Anglophone practitioners in the field typically thought women and gender and class together; among these are Leonore Davidoff and Catherine Hall, *Family Fortunes: Men and Women of the English Middle Class, 1780-1850* (London: Routledge, 1987); Angela Woollacott, *On Her Their Lives Depended: Munitions Workers in the First World War* (Berkeley: University of California Press, 1994); and Kathleen Brown, *Good Wives, Nasty Wenches, and Anxious Patriarchs: Gender, Race, and Power in Colonial Virginia* (Chapel Hill: University of North Carolina Press, 1996).

Masculinity was a critical site of investigation from the start: see John Tosh, *Manliness and Masculinities in Nineteenth-Century Britain* (London: Routledge, 1993); Mrinalini Sinha, *Colonial Masculinity: The "Manly Englishman" and the "Effeminate Bengali" in the Late Nineteenth Century* (Manchester, UK: Manchester University Press, 1995); and Robert Morrell, ed., *Changing Men in Southern Africa* (Pietermaritzburg, South Africa: University of Natal Press, 2001).

## Gender, sex, and feminist history

Joan Scott's *Gender and the Politics of History* (New York: Columbia University Press, 1988) was part of a quickly developing subfield in the discipline that insisted on gender as a category of historical analysis. Though each had their own journals, women, gender, and sexuality were most often interlinked, and among scholars of color interested in the histories of women of color, they were always cross-hatched by race and ethnicity, as with Teresa Barnes, *"We Women Worked So Hard": Gender, Urbanization, and Social Reproduction in Colonial Harare, Zimbabwe, 1930–1956* (Portsmouth, NH: Heinemann, 1999); Tera Hunter, *To 'Joy My Freedom: Southern Black Women's Lives and Labors after the Civil War* (Cambridge, MA: Harvard University Press, 1997); Catherine Ceniza Choy, *Empire of Care: Nursing and Migration in Filipino History* (Durham, NC: Duke University Press, 2003); and Brenda Child, *Holding Our World Together: Ojibwe Women and the Survival of Community* (New York: Penguin, 2012).

Denise Riley's *"Am I That Name?" Feminism and the Category of "Women" in History* (Basingstoke, UK: Macmillan, 1988) kept sex, feminism, and women together at the fore of theoretical debate, while histories of prostitution and deviance helped to reshape historiographies in the West (Judith Walkowitz, *Prostitution and Victorian Society* [Cambridge: Cambridge University Press, 1980]) and beyond (Laura Engelstein, *The Keys to Happiness: Sex and the Search for Modernity in Fin-de-Siècle Russia* [Ithaca, NY: Cornell University Press, 1992]).

Well before the institutionalization of global history, historians of gender were transnational in their thinking and in their investigation of the geographical specificity of how gender mattered; see Pete Sigal, *From Moon Goddesses to* Virgins (Austin: University of Texas Press, 2000) and Anna Clark, *Desire: A History of European Sexuality* (London: Routledge, 2019).

## Intersectionality

The key to intersectional theory and practice is Kimberlé Crenshaw's groundbreaking legal history article, "Demarginalizing the Intersection of Race and Sex: A Black Feminist Critique of Antidiscrimination Doctrine, Feminist Theory and Antiracist

Politics," *University of Chicago Legal Forum* 1, Article 8 (1989): 139–67. Intersectional histories clustered in several fields. Studies of slavery, led by Deborah Gray White (*Aren't I a Woman: Female Slaves in the Plantation South* [New York: W. W. Norton, 1985]), helmed this work, as did scholars of African American women (Darlene Clark Hine, *Hine Sight: Black Women and the Re-Construction of American History* [Bloomington: Indiana University Press, 1994]).

Feminist historians of the French Revolution were also in the vanguard; see, for example, Lynn Hunt, *The Family Romance of the French Revolution* (Berkeley: University of California Press, 1992) and Clare Haru Crowston, *Fabricating Women: The Seamstresses of Old Regime France, 1675–1791* (Durham, NC: Duke University Press, 2001).

And histories of imperialism pushed the boundaries of the rise of feminist research design and gendered findings, as seen in Philippa Levine, *Prostitution, Race, and Politics* (New York: Routledge, 2003) and Carina Ray, *Crossing the Color Line* (Athens: Ohio University Press, 2015).

Intersectional approaches carried into many terrains, as with Siobhan Somerville's *Queering the Color Line*, and into new institutional spaces, like the history of prisons, and of carcerality more generally; see Regina Kunzel, *Criminal Intimacy: Prison and the Uneven History of Modern American Sexuality* (Chicago: University of Chicago Press, 2008) and Talitha Leflouria, *Chained in Silence: Black Women and Convict Labor in the New South* (Chapel Hill: University of North Carolina Press, 2015).

The search for histories unseeable simply through the lens of gender and class called for new approaches to the archive, from Antoinette Burton's *Dwelling in the Archive* (Oxford: Oxford University Press, 2005) to Jennifer Morgan's *Laboring Women* (Philadelphia: University of Pennsylvania Press, 2004) to Marisa Fuentes's *Dispossessed Lives* (Philadelphia: University of Pennsylvania Press, 2018).

## Challenging Western modernity

Though more focused on sex than gender, Valerie Traub's *Thinking Sex with the Early Moderns* (Philadelphia: University of Pennsylvania Press, 2016) captures what scholars working in times and places before the modern strove to show from the very origins of the field: that gender was not universal across time and space, and that modernity itself had contributed to the hardening of the two-gender system.

Merry Wiesner-Hanks has done prodigious work in service of this claim across monographs and textbooks, including *Gender in History: Global Perspectives* (Chichester, UK: Wiley Blackwell, 2010) and *Christianity and Sexuality in the Early Modern World: Regulating Desire, Reforming Practice* (London: Routledge, 3rd edition, 2020), to name only a few of her publications. Medievalists, for their part, have pressed historians to see the way the distant past has been mapped onto so-called lesser civilizations; see Kathleen Davis and Nadia Altschul, eds., *Medievalisms in the Postcolonial World: The Idea of "the Middle Ages" Outside Europe* (Baltimore: Johns Hopkins University Press, 2010), which serves gender history well.

Afsaneh Najmabadi's *Women with Mustaches and Men without Beards: Gender and Sexual Anxieties of Iranian Modernity* (Berkeley: University of California Press, 2005) is an exemplary study in the decolonizing of gender history through a recognition of gender's unexamined universalist claims. Anjali Arondekar's *For the Record* (Durham, NC: Duke University Press, 2009) does similar work for sexuality and the colonial archive.

## Gender, queer, and trans history

The work of queer history has been practically coterminous with the professionalization of gender history across many time periods and geographies. Early titles include Caroline Dinshaw, *Getting Medieval: Sexualities and Communities, Pre- and Postmodern* (Durham, NC: Duke University Press, 1999); George Chauncey, *Gay New York: Gender, Urban Culture, and the Making of the Gay Male World, 1890–1940* (New York: Basic Books, 2005); Leila Rupp, *A Desired Past: A Short History of Same-Sex Love in America* (Chicago: University of Chicago Press, 1999); and Pete Sigal, *From Moon Goddesses to Virgins: The Colonization of Yucatecan Maya Sexual Desire* (Austin: University of Texas Press, 2000).

Susan Stryker has been a foundational figure in both transgender studies and transgender history: she edited *The Transgender Studies Reader* (New York: Routledge) in 2006 and wrote *Transgender History* for Seal Press in 2008. Other important titles are Emily Skidmore, *True Sex: The Lives of Trans Men at the Turn of the Twentieth Century* (New York: New York University Press, 2017) and Jen Manion, *Female Husbands: A Trans History* (Cambridge: Cambridge University Press, 2020).

Like gender history as a whole, scholarship investigating the queer and transgender past has aimed to be intersectional and global. Among the recent titles leading these efforts are C. Riley Snorton, *Black on Both Sides: A Racial History of Trans Identity* (Minneapolis: University of Minnesota Press, 2017); T. J. Tallie, *Queering Colonial Natal: Indigeneity and the Violence of Belonging in Southern Africa* (Minneapolis: University of Minnesota Press, 2019); and Howard Chiang, *Transtopia in the Sinophone Pacific* (New York: Columbia University Press, 2021).

# Index

Figures are indicated by an italic *f* following the para ID.

# SEXUALITY
## A Very Short Introduction
Veronique Mottier

What shapes our sexuality? Is it a product of our genes, or of society, culture, and politics? How have concepts of sexuality and sexual norms changed over time? How have feminist theories, religion, and HIV/AIDS affected our attitudes to sex? Focusing on the social, political, and psychological aspects of sexuality, this *Very Short Introduction* examines these questions and many more, exploring what shapes our sexuality, and how our attitudes to sex have in turn shaped the wider world. Revealing how our assumptions about what is 'normal' in sexuality have, in reality, varied widely across time and place, this book tackles the major topics and controversies that still confront us when issues of sex and sexuality are discussed: from sex education, HIV/AIDS, and eugenics, to religious doctrine, gay rights, and feminism.

www.oup.com/vsi

# WITCHCRAFT
## A Very Short Introduction
### Malcolm Gaskill

Witchcraft is a subject that fascinates us all, and everyone knows what a witch is - or do they? From childhood most of us develop a sense of the mysterious, malign person, usually an old woman. Historically, too, we recognize witch-hunting as a feature of pre-modern societies. But why do witches still feature so heavily in our cultures and consciousness? From Halloween to superstitions, and literary references such as Faust and even Harry Potter, witches still feature heavily in our society. In this Very Short Introduction Malcolm Gaskill challenges all of this, and argues that what we think we know is, in fact, wrong.

'Each chapter in this small but perfectly-formed book could be the jumping-off point for a year's stimulating reading. Buy it now.'

**Fortean Times**

www.oup.com/vsi